OLD MEN AND HORSES

A GIFT OF HORSEMANSHIP

OLD MEN AND HORSES

A GIFT OF HORSEMANSHIP

ROSS JACOBS

To my parents, Marie and Joe.

No son had it luckier.

CONTENTS

ACKNOWLEDGEMENTS

The first stories were initiated by a request from Di Politz who editor of the magazine, Chaff Chat. Since then Des Miller has taken the helm of the magazine and has been extremely supportive. Thank you Di and Des. I want to thank Pekka, and old friend who is no longer with us, but who got me started on this journey to have a better understanding of horses. My appreciation goes to Harry Whitney who has been one of my closest friends and mentor. Harry has been more generous with his time, advice and friendship that I could ever replay. He has also inspired several of the stories in the book. There is a quite a bit of Harry and Pekka in both Walt and Amos.

I want to thank Tom Moates, not only for his kind words in the fore-word, but because it was his enthusiasm for the stories and initiative that culminated in the compilation of the stories in this book.

Finally, my love and thanks to my wife, Michèle. She is my partner in every sense of the word and the love of my life. Her thoughtful criticisms and suggestions have made a significant impact on the final outcome of the book.

INTRODUCTION

"Cuppa?" Ross asked me in his Australian accent. I had no idea what he meant until he turned, brandishing a mug in one hand and a pot of coffee in the other.

"You bet, " I replied in my American tongue, twanged just a touch in my Virginia dialect.

Obviously, I was going to like this bloke. We just had met after my arrival in the kitchen of a bunk house in the desert near the town of Salome, Arizona.

Out there on that trip among a bunch of horses, the seguaro cacti, mesquite bushes, I first met Walt, Amos and the young narrator of this book. Now, that's not exactly true... and you figure it must be a lie since this book is a work of fiction, right?

Well, I was out west for the first time to see my friend and fantastic horseman, Harry Whitney. People trailered horse in from all over to his place for horsemanship clinics, and I'd been invited to come and watch. Ross and his wife, Michèle, long time friends of Harry's, also were there making an annual visit, working horses for a few folks and taking in the clinics.

I think it was Michèle who first mentioned Ross' stories and the trio of main characters. After more prodding from me over the course of a few days I discovered at least 30 of these stories already were written.

Some months after my return to Virginia, I received a smattering of these tales via e-mail. I sat down and read Ross' stories. Instantly I knew something truly unique and profound was in hand. So much really great and important information existed between the lines it shocked me. Not to mention, as a seasoned writer, I was instantly incredibly jealous of Ross' personal ability to spin a yarn; what dialog!

What follows in these pages is fantastic and not easily achieved. We the horse-obsessed are very fortunate Walt and Amos are horsemen rather than chefs, or firemen, or mechanics, or aviators. I don't know if Ross found it easy to weave these words onto the page, but when I read them, clearly, instantly, their value to our equestrian minded kind sprang out.

These stories needed to be bound between two covers for people to enjoy straight through. These characters needed a permanent home, preserved for posterity, in libraries and on bookshelves, because what they offer is insight into some of the most difficult aspects of horsemanship to comprehend. Some of the understanding gleaned by the reader in these stories may even be unattainable through non-fictional discourse.

Herein the reader finds wisdom in the form of story, and may discover that through osmosis, after reading evenly only a few of these chapters, some positive changes with equine relationships occur in a practical sense. And, these stories stick.

I think of it like this: Who forgets his first bicycle wreck with blood spattering everywhere, horrified onlooking friends freaking out, and the subsequent trip to the ER for stitches – and who (other than those that need it as a tool at work) remembers the Pythagorean Theorem from high school?

Good fiction is a bloody bicycle wreck, and good nonfiction always remains more of a cold calculation.

Stating facts and posing arguments, while academic and potentially wonderful explanatory, and perhaps even entertaining, lacks fiction's deeper resonance and meaning. It is fiction that can grip one right in the chest with both hands and shake the emotions up. Stirring fiction is hard, sometimes impossible, to forget. When there is an instructive by-product to such prose, its lessons are likewise difficult to misplace in the memory files.

Ross told me he receives letters sometimes from upset readers (who came to know Walt and Amos through magazine printings of some of these stories) who cannot, will not, be convinced that the characters are completely fictitious. There are no two old twin horsemen with outrageous accents lurking in Ross' past, but the reader's disbelief is so suspended by Ross' mastery of dialog and description that the reaction is symptomatic of the power wielded by an extraordinary writer.

It helps if the author, as in this case, is likewise an extraordinary horseman. Ross is just such a one, and he makes his living working to improve the horse's lot in this world. You may want to visit the web site that describes what he offers in the world beyond fiction: *http://www.goodhorsemansip.com.au/*.

As for the lessons-by-story... a living, breathing label seems to attach to them in our memories, stands out over all the chatter of other unemotional stored information, and they remain highlighted forever and easily retrieved as tools applied to life.

I suppose well done autobiography, though non-fiction, may bleed over into this category – but only when it reads like great fiction (and since such work is the memoir of the author's perspective, it may be *a whole lot* like fiction at times).

Academic literature is an intellectual pursuit – fictional prose, on the other hand, can pluck the nerves across the spectrum of human experience, from intellect to emotion.

Well developed characters, like us readers, really bleed when cut, if only in our minds. Their joys and sufferings are real in a virtual place inside of us, even if they are not true historical occurrences. Those experiences remain with us if the writer is truly gifted. Such characters change us. There are fictitious people who forever maintain my undying empathy, sometimes even more than the living, breathing variety I have met running around this earth.

On that list are such notables as King Arthur after Guinevere's betrayal, Levin as he grapples with life in Tolstoy's *Anna Karenina,* and even Hansel and Gretel, and Cinderella. Oh yeah... definitely Road Runner and Coyote, both.

Add to that list the old two old twins, Walt and Amos, and the young narrator of the didactic tales that unfold beyond this introduction. This book is unparalleled in the horse world. Nowhere else is such critically important information about getting better with horses more accessible, understandable, enjoyable, and presented in ways that remain woven in the fibers of memory as only fiction can.

A better way to approach horsemanship all makes sense and begins to take shape as the old fellers school the young boy through many tough spots. The truth is, one may not even realize the lessons that are there between the lies, and may just enjoy the stories. The wise old codgers don't tell the boy things… they give him plenty of rope to hang himself, and he does. Don't we all? I know I do. And we swing along with the boy in that noose. Then, Walt and Amos are there to gently offer a better option, a chair to stand on perhaps, if we'd like to consider it. The sage gentlemen don't grab the halter rope away and the lead the horse to show what needs to happen (we all know they can do it). They merely suggest we remove the noose from our necks, and use that rope differently, with the horse perhaps?

I am reminded, when I think of Ross' work, of what Mark Twain said somewhere. Between the lines, the quote just seems to sum up what I mean to say about this great book: *"When I was a boy of 14, my father was so ignorant that I could hardly stand to have the old man around. But when I got to be 21, I was astonished at how much the old man had learned in seven years."*

Tom Moates

PREFACE

This book is a collection of stories that I had written for Chaff Chat, which is the magazine published monthly by the Horse Riders Clubs Association of Victoria (HRCAV). At first I was unsure what I could possibly write about. I had written some training articles for a nationally published horse magazine in the past. But I have for a long time felt that the "how to" type of training article was extremely limited when it actually came to helping people.

I began thinking that perhaps there was a better way to help people than to simply telling them how to train a horse. I had read Mark Rashid's first book and thought the concept of a story with a message would be both entertaining and thought provoking. This is how the stories for *Chaff Chat* evolved.

Most of the stories involve the laconic twin brothers, Walt and Amos. In their early seventies, they have a wisdom regarding horses that few people ever achieve. Though they aren't identical, their leathery faces and slow demeanor confuse many characters in the stories. They are slow talking, but quick witted and relish a joke at my expense. They are extremely close. Neither Walt nor Amos ever tried to tell anyone what they should or should not do around a horse. Instead, they helped people in the way they helped horses. They shared their knowledge with those that wanted to know and allowed the individual to decide what to do with it. There was no force, no lecturing and no judgments made of either people or horses.

All the stories are inspired by real characters and real events even if the details may have been altered a little for the sake of the story. I am sure there are many Walt and Amos' in paddocks around the world who understand and get along with horses in ways the rest of us can only hope to achieve. It is to them and the people who strive each day to give their horses a better deal that this book is dedicated.

Ross Jacobs

IT'S NOT WHAT YOU DO,
BUT HOW YOU DO IT!

I was working at a riding school to earn extra money during the school holidays. I loved being around the horses. Most days were spent cleaning paddocks or stables and on really exciting days I got to clean saddlery. Most days were fairly quiet. The boss wasn't around too much and largely left me to get on with my jobs. A few boarders would show up now and then to ride their horses. The most regular clients were Walt and Amos. Walt and Amos were old timers and twin brothers. I was a young, brash teenager whom the old men had taken a liking to, and had offered me rides home in the evenings. They were smart around horses and knew more than anybody I had ever met. But there was more than that. Not only did they know more, they felt more. They weren't agile or quick on their feet; they had reached their physical peak as men many decades ago. Their weathered faces looked like crumpled brown paper framed in facial stubble. Walt was older than Amos by nearly an hour and as such Amos seemed to always look up to his big brother and echoed nearly everything Walt offered.

In the early days, there wasn't much chance of getting to ride at this job until a fellow called Bruce, who had been boarding at the riding school for about six months, asked me to ride his buckskin horse while he was away for a few weeks. He told me to watch her because she could be a little bad tempered when she was ridden. I wasn't worried because I had seen Bruce ride and knew I could handle anything he could.

A week later, Bruce had left town and his horse was all mine. After I finished all my jobs at the end of the day, I saddled her up. She seemed pretty quiet and friendly in the stable. I took her over to the arena and hopped on. Things were going pretty well as we walked around the arena. I did notice that every time I applied some leg pressure she would pin her ears back, but it didn't worry me too much. I figured she was trying to show me who was in charge. But I had my own opinion about who was the boss.

When I asked her to trot, she shook her head, pinned her ears and swished her tail. It seemed to me that her objection was nothing short of rudeness and I was not going to accept her rudeness. Besides, a cute girl with red hair was watching and I didn't want her to think I couldn't ride. I kicked the little mare in the ribs to insist on some respect. Her reaction caught me a bit by surprise. I remember a sense of floating and I remember a jolt, but exactly how I came to be on the ground was a mystery.

Covered in dust and sand I sat on the ground wondering what had happened a few microseconds beforehand. I saw a couple of figures walking towards me from across the other side of the arena. I must have taken quite a knock because it took me a moment to realize that it was Walt and Amos. But I couldn't mistake the trademark voice of Walt.

"Them bones of yours need gluin, son" asked Walt.

"Yeh, anythin rattlin that wernt rattlin before" asked Amos?

Both brothers were clearly quite amused by my misfortune. They helped me up, checked me over and walked away after they were convinced I was in one piece. The cute red haired girl delivered the buckskin over to me. I was too embarrassed to look her in the eye and just took the reins with a "thanks."

I got back on convinced I was going to teach the mare a lesson in manners. Even before my right foot was in the stirrup, I kicked her in the ribs with all my might. Her head spun around and she bit me on the lower calf. My yell was pure reflex. I kicked again and this time she charged off with her tail swished and her ears permanently flattened backwards.

I worked that little mare into a lather of sweat for an hour and half. I took her up and down the transitions like a music student doing scales. She never did lose her nasty expression and sometimes she still insisted on a pig root when I applied leg pressure. I was convinced this was the most spoilt, piggy horse I had ever ridden.

My own exhaustion was the determining factor when deciding to stop riding. I realized the mare was not much better now than when I began, but I was just too tired to keep going. After I had hosed her down, gave her some hay and put the gear away, I went to see Walt about a lift home.

"You've had a pretty excitin day," Walt observed. "I expect ya could do with a ride home. Too tired to walk I s'pose."

"Yeah," I said. "I'm pretty tired, but I wasn't going to let that mare get away with her nonsense. I think she knows that I won't take that stuff from her by now."

"Yeah, ya probably right," asked Walt? Tell ya what," he said. "Ya know that pocket knife I got that ya been tellin me ya admire so much? Well, if ya can get it out of me jacket pocket Amos and me will not only give ya a lift home, but give ya the knife for workin so hard with that mare."

He stood looking at me with his hands in his pockets. I made some remark about how silly this was, but I did like that knife and I really did want a lift home. I stepped forward and tried to lift his hand out of the pocket with the knife. It wouldn't move. I then tried to put my hand in the pocket to pick up the knife, but there wasn't enough room in the pocket for both our hands. I tried again even harder to get Walt's hand out of the pocket, but no luck. Frustrated and in no mood for this silly game, I gave up and said it was a stupid game.

Walt turned to Amos and said, " Amos, you try to get me knife out of me pocket. See if you can do better than Tarzan here."

Amos walked up to Walt and said, "Walt, would ya mind lendin me ya knife so I can open up that bale of hay to feed me horse, please?"

Walt took the watch out of his pocket. "Of course, Amos. Here ya go."

Walt then looked at me and said, "Looks like ya will be walkin, son. It's a good thing that little buckskin filly didn't have a knife in her pocket or ya'd been walkin around that arena on foot for more than an hour."

The brothers turned away and walked towards their car. I protested about them cheating me in their stupid game, but they pretended to be deaf.

As I made the long walk home, I fumed about Walt and Amos. Why had they played such a silly game? Why didn't they just give me a ride, like so many times before? And what was that remark about the horse having a knife in her pocket meant to be about? That seemed so stupid. The whole incident seemed stupid.

The next day I got a chance to ride the filly again. This time she started out even crankier than she was the previous day. Again, I worked her until we were both tired, but there was hardly an improvement in her attitude. In fact, she seemed even worse. I was beginning to feel frustrated with her and my leg was hurting even more from yesterday's bite.

Amos and Walt were not around that day, so I had to walk home again. The joke about the pocket knife was still bugging me. I figured there must have been a point to it. These guys were old, but not senile. Maybe they were trying to teach me a point. Old people seem to feel it's their duty to teach young people a lesson about something or other. I knew they were pretty handy around horses. Their own horses seem to really love them and would even lay down so the old boys could get on their backs without troubling their old bones. Both these fellows had such a good relationship with their horses and I think theirs were the happiest and best going horses on the property. Maybe Walt was trying to teach me a point about horses. Maybe it was a point about the buckskin mare!

These thoughts played in my mind over and over. How come Walt wouldn't let me take the knife out of his pocket, but when Amos asked him for the knife he gave it to him straight away? I guess I was a little rude to just try to grab the knife. It seemed Walt was ok to give Amos the knife when he asked. Maybe that was it. Maybe Walt was trying to tell me that if I was polite about something I am more likely to succeed than if I was rude.

The next day when I got a chance to saddle up the little mare, I decided I was going to try and ask for her to go forward and not demand it so forcefully. Maybe she was snitchy because I was being too hard on her. I had nothing to lose by trying a new approach since I had gotten nowhere in two days with a kick in the ribs.

At first I didn't get very far by asking politely. She still pinned her ears and squinted her eye. But I kept asking politely every time I wanted her to do something different. Pretty soon the mare didn't seem to mind too much. The tail was quieter and while her ears were focused on me they didn't seem annoyed with me. I figured that was enough improvement for one lesson and decided to cut the session short.

Over the next few weeks, that little buckskin mare got softer and happier and more responsive with each lesson. We were making a pretty good partnership and she seemed happier to see me each day. Even Walt commented, "She seems not to mind ya too much these days."

The unhappy part came when Bruce returned from his trip. He got on her and kicked her in the ribs to make her go and yanked the reins to make her stop or turn her around a corner. It took him maybe less than five minutes to undo the three weeks work I had put into her. It made me sad for her.

Bruce's mare, with the help of Walt and Amos, taught me a pretty important lesson about how a horse can reflect back at a person the same treatment that person gives to the horse. I learned that if I was rude to the horse, she was rude to me. But if I was polite to her, she did her best to be polite to me.

I decided that old Walt and Amos had a few things to teach me and I began to hang around them more and more. I was often the butt of their jokes, but they were kind to me and over the years they taught me more about how a horse thinks and feels than anyone else I ever knew. Even now, I hear them muttering at me whenever I get it wrong with a horse.

THE FIRST RIDE SHOULD
NEVER BE FOREVER

"Do ya reckin ya 'bout ready to start ya first horse?" Walt asked.

Walt and Amos had been given the job of breaking-in a skittish young filly. Amongst the locals they were considered a bit eccentric, but were known to be fine horsemen despite their years and stiff joints. Sometimes people would send a horse to the old men for help. On this occasion Walt had hinted that I could help to get the filly started. I had seen the fellows start a few young ones, but I was pretty nervous about my first one.

Walt was sitting on his little bay filly looking down at me. "Makin a bad horse don't take no effort," he wiped his brow, "gettin a good un always takes a bit of thought and some bit of understanding. Ya do that and you'll do ok." He turned away to leave me and the young horse alone in the round yard.

I could fill a book with the stories of the first time I broke in that horse. Every day would be a chapter. Walt and Amos made me feel I was doing it all on my own, but when I look back there was always a guiding hand coming from the shadows. I don't think they ever let me get into hot water and in a sort of non-interfering way they made sure I kept on the right side of trouble. I learned so much each day that I was forgetting some stuff as quick as other stuff was being absorbed.

One of the things that made a huge impression on me and has lasted to this day happened on the first ride. I did a lot of preparation in the last few weeks before I felt good enough to get on for the first ride. In the beginning, the filly came to me very nervous and suspicious of most things I tried to do with her, but we had come a long way and with Walt's prompting I felt the big day had come. Despite all the preparation, I was still feeling weak at the thought of sitting atop and images of riding a tornado kept passing through my mind.

With some trepidation and help from Walt I prepared to mount. I slapped the stirrups; I put a foot in and out of the stirrups several times. I put weight in the stirrups and made out as if I was about to mount her a few times. She took to this pretty well. I kept thinking I had better do some more of this sort of stuff until Walt chided me, "Are you ever goin to get on?" So I did.

I sat calmly into the saddle wondering what to do next. It was quickly obvious that the filly was not going to buck. Well, not immediately. In fact, the opposite was the problem. All four feet seem to be stuck to the earth. Walt guided me through freeing the horse's feet using only rein and no leg. He suggested using one rein to get the horse to turn its head slightly then wait until the feet followed. Once the feet moved I let the rein go and did nothing until the feet stopped again. Then I used the other rein and repeated the process. It didn't take very long before the horse just walked wherever the reins took her.

I was feeling pretty good about how things were going. I kept moving the young filly around the yard and she seemed quiet and relaxed. However, after a little time the filly seemed to get harder to move again. When I asked her to turn, she would take a step and stop. Ask for another turn, she'd stop again. This time I got a little more insistent because she seemed to be trying to take over. Instead of letting the reins go when she moved her feet, I kept turning her to keep them moving. But this wasn't helping at all. In fact, I felt her get very braced in her back and before I knew it she was bucking and turning like she was having a fit. This is when I learned just how athletic a horse she could be. I landed on a soft patch, but not soft enough to prevent it hurting. Worse still, Walt just sat on the fence looking at the palm of his hand as he picked at a splinter and didn't say a word. I knew that meant I had done something stupid.

"I did'n think ya was ever goin to get off," was the comment from the fence. "I'd 'ave thought ya had gone up there for a vacation and weren't expectin ya back for another week or two." Walt still hadn't looked up from picking at his splinter.

I collected myself together again, dusted off my clothes and walked over to the filly. She was a little shaken, but not as much as me. I figured I had to get back on her and ride her some more so she wouldn't learn that bucking got her out of work. I put my foot in the stirrup and swung a leg over as carefully as I could and sat down in the saddle. I began to pick up a rein, but Walt's voice stopped me.

"Good. That'll do. Now ya had ya second ride, let it finish better than the first. Get off and put her away."

"But Walt, I haven't got her moving yet. Shouldn't I get her moving again before I finish?"

"Ya on her ain't ya? She's not buckin is she? Ya already doin better than the last ride. I think it might be a good spot to finish before she starts to think about a buck. Or do ya like the taste of dirt so much?"

I shut up and did what Walt suggested. It was clear he knew something I didn't and he was looking out for me and the filly.

I later asked Walt why the filly got more resistant and finally bucked and twisted.

"Well, maybe she was gettin in a bind." he replied. "She might've been thinkin that every time she went along with ya suggestin of movin, ya just kept askin for her to move again. Maybe she figured there was no way out for her. Ya did good to begin, but then you kept askin for more. How was she to know ya'd ever stop askin?"

I thought about this for awhile. It was like a lightning bolt. The filly had no idea that I was going to get off her in a few minutes and put her away for a rest. As far as she was concerned I had got on her back and I was going to be there for life and there was no way out for her. At first she tried really hard to cope, but when she was getting no relief, she couldn't tolerate it anymore and had to do something. So she bucked. I caused her to buck by staying up there too long and asking too much for where she was today. Walt must have seen it happening, but didn't say anything. He figured I had an important lesson to learn.

Over time, the importance of that lesson was obvious in everything I did with a horse. It is still the case. Horses live in the moment. They have no sense of time. They learn by association. When I get on a horse for the first time, he doesn't know that I will ever get off. But if I get on and get off soon after, he can learn to associate that I will not be up there forever. The same is true if I put a horse in a float, or ask him to lunge or pick up a foot. If the horse hasn't learned by association that it is not forever, he could well panic and do whatever he thinks he needs to do to get out of the situation. It's self-preservation taking over. The same sense of self-preservation that you would have if I locked you in a cupboard and you didn't know that I would let you out in thirty seconds.

I learned from Walt and Amos that if you want a horse to trust you, don't just force him to accept things. Let him learn that you will find him a way out of his dilemma. You will make sure that his problem is not forever. As Walt told me once, "We are goin to show him what we want to do, and we are goin to show him that it's just temporary."

WHAT MAKES A
GOOD LEADER?

When I was a teenager, I had a riding friend Dave Reinhardt, whose father had just bought a gelding ready for breaking-in. Dave's dad figured he'd get the horse cheaper if it was unbroken and then he'd do the job himself. Mr. Reinhardt had started a few horses in his younger days and had been attending some clinics and seminars of a couple of the more popular horse trainers to visit the region in recent months. Dave told me his dad was all fired up about this new stuff he had been learning and couldn't wait to start his new horse.

Besides Walt and Amos, I hadn't seen another person break in a horse before. I was keen to see how somebody else would go about it, since it was entirely possible that Walt and Amos didn't know everything about horses. Wouldn't it have been a hoot if I could learn something new from Mr. Reinhardt and then show the old brothers that I knew something they didn't? I managed to wangle myself an invitation to watch Dave's dad on the first day with the new horse.

It was very clear from the start that Mr. Reinhardt loved an audience. He talked an awful lot about horses. In fact, he talked so much he didn't get too much done with the horse. He went on and on about how his new horse was pushy and rude and needed to be taught respect. Mr. Reinhardt said that he learned from these other trainers that the best way to teach a horse respect is to act like you are the boss of the herd. He said that a horse respects a more dominant horse, so if you present yourself as the dominant member of the herd you'd get a horse to respect you. He said this meant that he needed to assert his dominance over the horse with such things as being firm about the horse not invading his space and being firm about not allowing the horse to nip at him and being firm about the horse stopping when asked to stop. In this way the horse would know who was boss and therefore respect and obey Mr. Reinhardt much more.

I watched Dave's dad work the horse on the ground and heard him continue to rabbit on about dominance and submission. His horse was very pushy and really didn't lead well. Mr. Reinhardt got pretty firm about not letting his horse walk over him. Every time the horse transgressed into Mr. Reinhardt's space the lead rope would come swinging in the air to drive the horse away. When Mr. Reinhardt would ask his new horse to take a step back and he would shake the lead rope under the chin like the rope was caught in a blender. Watching all this going on made me think a bit because while I liked Mr. Reinhardt's theory of presenting myself like a herd boss, it seemed the young horse before me didn't like it too much. What started out as a quiet, pushy horse was now becoming an obedient but worried horse. Whenever Mr. Reinhardt asked the horse to do something, the horse had a frightened and tense look about him. He would react or over react in a tight and braced fashion. Dave's dad seemed well pleased that his horse was now doing what it was told, but I felt uneasy about how the horse was doing what he was told. I had never seen Walt and Amos make such a quiet horse so tense, yet their horses were always so well mannered. I knew that to the old men it was just as important that a horse felt good about doing what was asked, as it was to actually do what was asked. They seem to take as much care of the inside of the horse as they did to whatever job the horse was doing. It was a struggle for me to understand what Mr. Reinhardt was showing me in light of what Walt and Amos had shown me.

I thought on this dilemma in the days that followed, but I wasn't making much headway in my thinking. I decided to ask Walt about it.

"Walt, Mr. Reinhardt was showing me the other day that you need to present yourself as a herd boss in order to get respect from a horse. He reckons that once you show a horse that you can be a bigger boss in the herd than he can, he will show you submission and respect."

Walt's only response was "Is that right?"

"Yeah. But when he showed me how to do this it seemed like his horse was getting more and more anxious. The horse certainly got submissive and polite, but he seemed really worried about a lot of things. Why did that happen?"

"How long does it take ya to clean out them stables for me an' Amos?"

"Umm. About 40 or 45 minutes. Why?"

"Well matey, for the next week ya can forget about cleanin them stables and instead I want ya to go down to the big paddock and study them 20 or so horses for 45 minutes every day. Me and Amos will worry 'bout those stables."

"But Walt, I don't understand!"

"If ya wanna know about herd bosses and herd behavior, ya might as well learn from the experts."

The way that Walt had said it I took as more of an order than a suggestion. Each afternoon I went and sat on the hill and stared down at the paddock. I didn't know what I was supposed to be looking at, but I guessed I should try and understand how the herd boss acted toward the others. It didn't take long to identify who was in charge of the mob. He was a big brown thoroughbred. Whenever he approached another horse, he pinned his ears and got them to move off. If they were a little slow to move he got pretty assertive about it until they did move. It seemed like he had them all bluffed.

After a couple of days of watching the herd I realized something else about the boss horse. Hardly any of the other horses hung out with him. There was a small group of 2 or 3 horses who tended to follow him around like lieutenants or gang members, but the other 15 or so horses had a habit of hanging around some small distance from the boss and his mates. The only time the other horses interacted with the boss was when he made overtures to them. There was very little attempt by a subordinate horse to make contact with the boss. It was almost like there were two herds. There was one other obvious aspect of this hierarchical system that I noticed by the end of the week. The second and larger herd had its own boss horse. He was still submissive to the big thoroughbred, but he seemed to be leader of the other 15 horses. What was even more intriguing was that the boss of the second herd did not seem to pin his ears or bare his teeth or use any other threatening gestures to influence the movement of horses in his group. He seemed to exert his dominance in an entirely different way to the thoroughbred. But I didn't understand how he did this. If he moved toward another horse, the horse simply stepped out of the way like he was being asked to make a little room, please. There was none of the aggression or scooting out of the way that characterized the interaction between the thoroughbred and the other horses. If the boss of the second group went somewhere the others followed like they were going on a picnic. It was very strange to me and I knew I had to talk to Walt if I was ever going to understand how the boss of the second herd established his leadership.

"Well, that big 'ol thoroughbred, he's a bit like them school bullies. Everybody is afraid of them 'cause they can be mean, but nobody wants be 'round them. Those other horses just does as he say 'cause they wanna stay outa trouble. And that thoroughbred needs to be mean 'cause he ain't got respect from those other horses. He just leads by intimidatin them.

"On the other hand, that horse in the second mob he don't need to intimidate nobody. He's got the others respectin him 'cause he is smart and easy to get along. The others know he can be mean if he has to, but he ain't have to too often. When anotha horse shows him respect, he shows them respect back. So they get along pretty good. But the thoroughbred never shows nobody any respect. The others do what he says and show him obedience, but they sure resent him. They'd much prefer bein with the other horse 'cause he shows them a betta kinda leadership.

"Doin too little gets nothin done. Doin too much gets less than nothin done. Now ya give that some thought next time ya askin a horse for respect before ya decide on what kinda herd boss ya wanna be."

I did give it some thought. As a matter of fact, I experimented with trying to be a respectful leader for years to come. It was a real struggle to get the balance just right between being a demanding boss and being a benevolent leader. Sometimes I was too passive and a horse would get confused about his role in the relationship and start to take over. Other times I was too bossy and a horse would become more submissive and obedient, but with that he would sometimes become tense and worried and lose the desire to want to work. For a long time I struggled with the notion of how much is too much and how much is not enough. Then I realized where I was going wrong. I was working too hard at what kind of boss I should be. What I really needed was to just work at filling in the spots where the horse needed help. I discovered that if I thought of it as more directing the horse to find a good place to be inside of himself; just guiding him through the trouble instead of trying to make the horse give me the response I wanted, and things got a lot better between us. As I became more aware of what the horses were feeling inside I eventually tuned in to how to be a leader that felt good to the horse. I found horses began to look to me for help when they were in a bother instead of automatically escaping from trouble. I found the difficult to catch horses became less difficult to catch and the snitchy horses became less snitchy. The nervous horses gained more confidence and the bossy horses gained more respect. It was a revelation to learn how to have a horse respectful, polite and obedient, yet still maintain the quality of leadership that made each horse a willing partner rather than a slavish employee.

Walt once said to me that he tried to treat each horse he met as if he knew that when his judgment day came, sitting on the throne in heaven would be that same horse. I thought back to horses that I had worked and felt a chill up my spine.

IF I HAD A HAMMER......

When I was a kid I collected all the horse magazines I could afford. I was so hungry for more information that I would devour anything and everything horsey. At the time, "Hoofs and Horns" was the most popular magazine on the newsagents rack. In those days it was published out of South Australia and contained everything from show results to rodeo reports. Occasionally they would publish an article on training techniques and how to fix a problem. These were always my favourite sections. Sometimes I would get the chance to try out the things described in the articles in my spare time at the riding school. There was one time I particularly remember that proved to be a more important lesson than I could have imagined.

The article in question was a description on how to solve the problem of a horse pulling back when tied up. This article took my interest because of one horse that was boarded at the riding school that always pulled back and broke the halter, lead rope or hitching rail. The owner would whack it every time it tried to pull back, but the horse never learned not to pull. The article described how to fit a Hessian bag around the horse's neck, behind the poll. A strong rope was attached to the ends of the bag with a special knot and the rope then fixed to a ring on a large, solid post. The ring could swivel so as the horse moved around, the ring would always rotate in the same direction. This prevented the rope from wrapping around the post. Also the ring was about six feet off the ground. After some thought I figured I could easily adapt some of the gear at the riding school to make a similar setup. The article even went onto to describe how you should let the horse pull against the rope and throw plastic buckets and empty feed bags at the feet of the horse to cause him to pull away. The theory was that eventually the horse would learn that pulling back was a waste of time and then submit to standing quietly. This all seemed fair enough to me and I decided to approach the owner of the horse to get permission to try and solve the problem.

The owner was very agreeable to the idea, so I went to work fitting a swivel ring to the big post that was in the jumping paddock. When that was done, I lead the horse to the post, slipped the folded Hessian bag over his neck and tied the strongest rope I could find. When everything was ready I stepped back and waited. Nothing happened for a few moments, but then the dust began to fly. The horse pulled and pulled, leapt forward and then pulled again. The rope, the bag, the halter and the post were still holding, but the horse was showing no signs of giving up. The more he pulled the more panicked he became. He threw himself around and only the shortness of the rope prevented him from falling to the ground a couple of times. I did not feel this was going well and I was beginning to sense some panic in myself too. Finally, the horse just stopped and leaned with all his weight against the rope – it was the only thing holding him up. He was not thrashing anymore, but his eyes began to close and I got a really bad feeling that this was not a good thing. I began to feel as scared as the horse and all I could hear was the pounding of my heart.

Suddenly I became aware of a voice behind me. I looked around and it was Walt shouting at me from the fence. He looked panicked too as if he had been trying to get my attention for awhile. I could just make out his words, "cut him loose, cut him loose." And then I saw a pen knife come sailing through the air from the arm of the old man. I ran to where it fell and opened the biggest blade. I ran back to the horse and tried to saw through the rope before the horse began to thrash again. When the rope was cut, the horse fell backwards and was on the ground. He lay there quietly. I felt sick. What had I done? I nearly killed him!

When Walt reached me the horse was still on the ground. He clipped a lead rope to the horse's halter and checked the horse for any injury. When satisfied that the horse was ok, Walt stood up and gave the horse a quick and firm kick to the belly. The shock of this had the horse standing quietly in an instant. I was expecting a terrible dressing down by Walt, but I think the look on my face told him to leave that for later. Instead, he told me to hose the horse down, give him some hay and put him in the paddock.

Later that day I was cleaning stables. I was still traumatized by the idea that I nearly killed a horse. I couldn't believe my stupidity. How did I ever think I knew enough to deal with such a problem? As I was shoveling wet sawdust, I heard the familiar voice of the old man.

"Well matey, did ya learn anythin this mornin?"

I could hardly look at Walt. As I answered him it was taking all my strength to hold back the tears.

"I learned how stupid I am. I learned that I have no right to ever go near another horse. I learned that I don't have a clue about horses."

"Well matey, there was a few lessons for ya to learn today. Never have a rope around a horse if ya ain't got a knife. Don't go tryin somethin new if there ain't nobody around who knows better. Just 'cause somethin is written in a book don't make it true. And don't use a hammer when ya's tryin to drive a screw into somethin."

That last bit caught me off guard. What did Walt mean about the hammer and the screw?

"Well matey, if ya give a man hammer who don't know nothin about carpentry he's likely to think that everythin looks like a nail."

"I don't get it Walt," I proclaimed.

"Well matey, I seen ya reading that magazine paper during ya lunch break. I know where ya got the idea from to fix that horse from pullin. And I know that you were tryin to do the right thing. But ya took the idea in the paper to be the answer to every horse that pulls back. The idea in the paper became ya hammer and the horse started to look like a nail. So ya pounded on the nail and didn't stop to ask if maybe the horse was really more like a screw and needed a screw driver or maybe he just needed a touch of glue."

"So Walt, are you saying that article was wrong?"

"Well matey, the fellow who wrote the article didn't know the horse you was workin on. How would he know that his method would work or not? It weren't his job to know about your horse. It was yours. I ain't blamin him. His horse might've acted like a nail, so probably a hammer is what he needed. But that little horse today weren't no nail and he needed somethin else. But ya didn't stop to think. You had a horse with a problem and ya had a hammer to fix it with. That's all ya took the time to think about.

"What should I have done then, Walt?"

"Well matey, that little horse is pretty tightly wound. My guess is that the problem is not so much with bein tied up, but with not bein able to escape if he feels the need. He gets scared about bein confined. If a big ol' scary thing jumps out at him, he wants to be sure he can get away. So when ya tie him up or put him in a horse float or get him to walk through a small gate, he gets bothered. Maybe ya should have been lookin for ways to help him get less bothered about bein confined instead of forcin him to do somethin that scared the colour out of his coat."

Once again Walt was right. I didn't stop to think and analyze the best way to handle the problem for the horse. The article told me how to use a hammer. So instead of seeing a horse with specific problem and specific solution, I just saw a nail. Thankfully I learned that lesson before I nearly killed another horse.

A LIFE TIME OF LEARNING

I had been working at the riding school for quite awhile. Even though I was only in my late teens, I figured hanging around horses and horsemen for this long qualified me to be a member of an elite group of the horseman's fraternity. It's not that I thought I knew everything there was to know. It's just that I considered myself to have better than average skills around horses and hanging around Walt and Amos gave me a breadth of experience with difficult horses that most other people at the riding school hadn't acquired.

I had seen horses with hard mouths get fixed. Horses that bolt get fixed. Horses that buck get fixed. Horses that shied get fixed. Horses that couldn't take a correct canter lead get fixed. I had seen the tricks to fixing all the little problems that horse people face at some time or other. I even remember Walt fixing a horse that used to lie down when taken out for a ride. I learned that if you let the horse lay down, then hobbled him so he couldn't get up and wait under a shady tree for an hour or so the problem would get fixed. It seemed to me that I had seen almost every problem that horses exhibit and I had seen how Walt and Amos fixed the problem. Walt and Amos had shown me all their secrets. I felt part of their club because clearly the three of us knew stuff about horses and training that none of the other people at the riding school knew. Even though these twin brothers were really old, they were cool when it came to knowing about horses and I was now learning that I was cool for being around them.

Being cool around horses was important to me because my mates at school used to give me a hard time for being interested in horses. To them horses were only taken seriously by girls. It was a sport for sissies as far as they were concerned. This used to get to me until one day my dad explained it to me.

"You have a choice, son. You can be with your mates on Saturday getting your head punched in as you pack down into a scrum or you can go to the riding school and be surrounded all day by cute girls in tight jodhpurs and get paid for it."

My father's logic could not be denied. I stuck with the horses and the cute girls. But in order to be of interest to the cute girls I had to be good around horses and that's why it was so cool to be adopted by Walt and Amos as a defacto apprentice. They were the wizards and I was their apprentice! Well, that's how I liked to see it. In hindsight, I'm not sure they felt the same way. I think I was more of a pesky pup to them. Nevertheless, they were kind and charitable with their time and their knowledge.

One day Walt poked his head into the stall I was cleaning. "A lady dropped off a gray Arab durin' the week, Ross. He's a bit shy 'bout lettin ya get a halter on him," he said. "How'd ya like to handle him for us? Me and Amos might be bit busy keepin that pack of girls away from ya to have time for this one."

Walt's joke did not go unnoticed, but this was a chance to handle a new horse and establish myself as a card-carrying member the cool club even further. I had seen Walt and Amos teach horses to be caught before, so I was pretty confident I could do the job. Previously, whenever the brothers got a horse that wandered away when they approached with a halter, they would encourage the horse to move away at a slightly faster pace than the horse intended to go. They didn't let the horse stop moving until it showed the smallest sign that it was interested in standing still. The idea was to try and make the option of being hard to catch a less comfortable choice than standing still. If the horse wandered out of range from the catcher, they would get the horse to expend a little more energy than he wanted until he decided it was easier to be caught. The brothers never chased a horse or drove it around until it was tired. They just made it a little hard for the horse to move out of range then stop for a rest, then move again and stop again. It was a game lots of horses liked to play and most people played the game according to the horse's rules. But Walt and Amos played the game to a different set of rules than most people and horses soon learned that life was much more comfortable if they stood and waited to be caught.

Knowing all this gave me the confidence to tackle the task that Walt had set me. I was going to teach the little Arab to be easy to catch. Walt had told me that he had put the horse in the round yard about half an hour ago and it was waiting for the first lesson. It didn't even occur to me until later that Walt had already caught the horse. How else did he get him into the round yard?

I stepped into the round yard with a halter and lead rope over my arm. The horse was on the far side of the yard with his head sticking over the top of the six-foot fence. This horse knew I was there, but I figured it had chosen to ignore me. I decided I should make my presence known in no uncertain terms. I stepped confidently toward the tail that was facing me and slapped the halter against my thigh. There was a "thwack" sound of the rope hitting my leg followed by a flurry of legs and hooves trying to climb out over the top of the fence. The Arab got a front leg caught between the top rail and next one down. He pulled back flexing his hocks as much as they would allow and managed to free himself with a thud as he landed on his backside. The panic continued as he scrambled to his feet and fled around the yard. There was a blank look on his face, but his body was running on turbo-charged adrenalin. I tried to block the Arab and send him in the other direction in order to break the mindless panic, but he was totally tuned out and bolted past.

On the way, he managed to knock me to the ground with his shoulder. It took me a little while to gather myself and I didn't look up until I was just about on my feet. What I saw was an angry gray gelding with ears pinned, teeth bared and front feet charging straight for me. Now it was my turn to panic. I scrambled toward the fence and leapt more than halfway up the wall in a single stride. But the horse was able to leave a tattoo in the shape of his teeth on my lower thigh before I hauled myself over the top of the fence.

Walt had seen the whole thing. I shouldn't have been surprised to see him with his boot propped on the bottom rail of the round yard. He grinned. "I guess ya showed him what were what, eh! Ya might wanna get ya self a change of unda pants before that little red haired girl smells ya." I was about to complain that the Arab was crazy and the meanest horse on the planet, but Walt got in before me.

"That poor horse. Ya scared him to death. He must've have figured ya was crazy and the meanest person on the planet."

"Why did he charge me, Walt?"

"I reckin ya might put up a fight if ya thought some one was tryin to kill ya too"

As he said that, Walt turned his back and walked away. I thought about what he said. Did the Arab really think his life was in danger? That would explain the panic and the bolting. Why didn't I see that before I jumped into that yard ready to drive that horse away? All the horses I had seen Walt and Amos teach to be caught had been playing at being hard to catch. But this horse was different. He was genuinely afraid to be caught. Moving him as I did just confirmed in him that life with people was awfully difficult, and I didn't help. He needed comfort and safety. He needed to feel it was ok for me to be just in the same yard as him, let alone caught by me. I felt so stupid for not seeing what was so obvious. This poor fellow was terrified and I treated him like he was a cheeky little pony.

This episode bothered me for days and I couldn't make myself go near the little Arab. It was obvious that I had not even attempted to work out the source of this horse's problem. I just assumed it was like all the others I had seen the old men train to be caught. I felt so inadequate and incompetent about my abilities with horses. I brooded about what had happened for days. My parents noticed something was wrong, but I couldn't explain it to them. It was a rude awakening to discover that I really knew nothing about horses when I had come to believe I was pretty handy around them. It was so depressing. I had no right to feel cool or even to be part of the same club as Walt and Amos. So you can imagine my surprise when Walt asked me, "Aren't ya ever goin to learn that horse to get caught?"

"I don't think I can Walt. I'll mess it up and make him even worse."

"I reckin ya know somethin ya didn't know before. Stop feelin sorry for yaself. So ya acted like a fox in a chook yard. Get in there and make things right with that horse. Ya'll do ok."

"How can I learn what you and Amos know about horses? How did you and Amos learn so much."

"We learned what we learned by gettin into trouble. Ya don't learn nothin from nothin goin wrong. Ya only get good with horses by makin mistakes with 'em and knowin ya did wrong."

"But how can you tell when you are on the right track," I asked?

"Ya gotta know what ya wanna happen and learn from the master."

"Master?"

"Out of me, you and that Arab who knows more 'bout what needs doin to make him wanna be caught?"

That got me thinking that maybe I needed to become a better listener instead of a talker when conversing with horses. Then Walt must have seen my despair because he added, "Don't let ya mistakes eat at ya, matey. It takes a life time to learn a life times worth of learnin. I ain't known nobody who has lived a life time - not even Amos." Walt winked and turned away.

STOP TALKING AND
START LISTENING

I am sometimes asked what is the most important thing that a person can learn about a horse? For a long time I would respond with answers like learning to have an independent seat or understanding that tension is the enemy of good training or that you can't do much until your horse learns to focus. But after giving it more and more thought I realized that while all these things were true, they stem from factors that are even more basic. What is even more basic to getting along with horses is in having an understanding of what a horse thinks and feels. For a person to develop this important skill requires a level of awareness of horse language that most of us tend to ignore. You can't even begin to understand things from the horse's point of view until your ability to listen to them becomes highly tuned. I'm not even talking about the obvious stuff like tail swishing, pinning of the ears or flinging of the head. Sometimes a yawn or a sneeze or minute shift in posture tells a tale about what a horse is feeling. Many years back I was taught this in a rather rude way by a smart young horse and a sly old man.

The horse's name was Cherry and it was a deep red chestnut thoroughbred mare. She was a horse Walt and Amos had picked up at a sale, and they gave her as a project. I didn't know much about this horse, but Walt told me it was pretty troubled and prone to bucking.

When I first began playing around with her she seemed pretty quiet but perhaps a little aloof. I got her saddled and hopped aboard. We rode around the arena for awhile. I asked for upward and downward transitions, change of directions and hindquarter yields. Cherry seemed to accept all of it, but she was a bit stiff through her body and wasn't terribly light on the reins. I had been riding Cherry for about 20 minutes and was just beginning the second loop of a three loop serpentine, when out of nowhere she dropped her head and bucked up a storm. I was so shocked and caught unaware that I think I only managed to stay in the saddle for the first two bucks. I think I recall that Cherry stopped and stood quietly after my face plowed into the dirt. It was such a surprise to me that I was a little shaken. I couldn't understand why she had done that and just assumed that there must have been something that happened in the corner of her eye that I didn't see that caused her to be set off like that. I got back on and rode for a few more minutes to make sure this would not become a habit.

Later that day I mentioned the incident to Walt. As usual, I found out that I didn't really have to because he had seen the whole thing. I had learned that it was rare that either Walt or Amos or both were not watching me from some hidden away location when they thought I might be working a horse that could give me a challenge. Walt said that I was probably right that the bucking was caused by a fright she got from a bird or something in a tree, but that maybe he would come along and have a look next time just to see how I was getting along with the mare.

The next ride was a couple of days later and Walt was a passive spectator leaning against a corner rail. This session started out pretty much as the previous one had done and I was feeling my confidence returning. At one point about 15 minutes into the workout I asked Cherry to canter out of a corner. She didn't really make it into a canter and I didn't quite make it out of the corner. The little red mare bucked and twisted so big that it loosened several filings in my back teeth. Luckily this time I happened to be in a position that had me landing feet first and rolling on my side, which prevented any serious injury. There was no more damage than a bruised ego and my legs metamorphosed into jelly.

When I finally gathered myself and caught the mare, I wandered over to Walt, who was examining the veins on the back of his leathery hand.

"Why did she do that, Walt?" I asked. "It seem to happen for no reason. Everything was fine and then she just exploded out of nowhere. Just like the other day."

"Did I ever tell ya 'bout me dad's dogs?" he asked me.

"Oh no," I thought to myself. "Here comes another one of Walt's stories. Why can't he just give me a straight answer to a straight question?" Walt didn't even wait for me to answer his question. He just kept on talking.

"Dad had a greyhound that he used for huntin. He was called Benny. He was a beauty and every mornin Dad would come out the back door off the kitchen and Benny'd come trottin over to 'im ready to go rabbitin for the mornin. As soon as that dog heard the squeak of that back door he'd be on his feet ready to go. But Benny had to go past Pav. Pav was a young kelpie dog that was chained up between the house and the kennel that dad had built for Benny. So Benny'd head towards the house in the mornin and past Pav within a couple of yards of the end of the chain. Pav would rush at Benny every day and yap his head off, but Benny seemed to pretty much ignore the commotion and trot past on his way to meet Dad. This was something that happened almost every day for about four years. Then one day Dad came out the back door, Benny got up and headed towards the house. He went past Pav and just like every other day Pav rushed to the end of his chain and barked wildly at Benny. Benny seemed to ignore it as usual and passed Pav without even seemin to see him. After Benny had gone a few yards he stopped, turned around and charged at Pav. By the time Dad had got there, Benny had already killed that little kelpie. Dad said he didn't understand it because Benny had never been vicious and the attack seem to come from nowhere. But ya know what matey, Benny had been thinkin about killin that kelpie for four years. It didn't come from nowhere, it just took all them years for Benny to let go of his self control. Now this little mare ya been on might have a touch of greyhound in her. Do ya think?"

"So Walt, are you saying that Cherry has been thinking about bucking me off ever since I got on her today?" I asked.

"Could be," he said. "D'ya see how she tries to avoid ya when you do somethin?"

"Umm, sort of," I said.

"Go up to her, matey and pat her on the forehead," Walt instructed. I did as he said.

"There! D'ya see that?"

"See what, Walt," I asked?

"Did ya notice that as you went to raise your hand near her forehead, this ol' mare turned to look sideways just a bit?"

I repeated the process and the mare did just as Walt said. I was beginning to wonder how come I didn't notice that before.

"Ya see matey, this mare ain't feelin too good about humans and would rather avoid 'em. It ain't your fault. I reckon she's been like this for a long time. But ya ain't helping her to feel better either. Seems to me that as soon as you get on her she starts talkin to ya about how she's feelin. Her head ain't never still for too long and did ya notice how she yawned a lot for a little while and when ya asked for a stop she more often than not would stretch her neck into them reins? Well, she was tryin to tell ya something, but you wouldn't listen. I guess she could only take so much of ya ignoring her concerns and she decided to take matters into her own hands to find relief. That's when she decided to help ya look for earthworms."

That night I thought a lot about what Walt had said. He had seen behaviour in Cherry that I had missed and that's what got me into trouble. Walt's level of awareness was so much more highly tuned than mine, but I made it a mission to get better. It is still a mission to get better. And it will always be a mission to get better. Walt later told me that most horse people spend a lifetime learning to be better riders and give more accurate riding aids, but hardly anytime in learning to feel of their horses. He said, "It's just as important to be a good listener as it is to be a good talker."

THE STORY OF KERO

I guess I was pretty arrogant in my early teens when it came to horses. In the beginning, I never used to worry about how a horse felt about being around me or working for me. I figured as long as I had a "whoa" a "go" and a "go this way" I was pretty good with horses. And I had the ribbons and competition prizes to prove it. Even the tough horses weren't taking me too much time to figure out and get going well enough to please their owners and do ok in competition. As the years passed, I began to discover (with the help of Walt and Amos) that it was a good idea to think more about the horses and what made them tick But even then, I had a peg or two knocked out of me when I met Kero.

Kero was a finely built gelding. He had been owned by a fellow who could no longer handle his hotness and had given him to Amos. The fellow was so relieved at never having to ride Kero again that he gave him to Amos as a gift. Like all horses, Kero basically had a good nature but suffered from "ants-in-the-pants" syndrome and the need to travel at speed no matter what he was doing. If you tried to slow him up he would carry on like the proverbial pork job and try to unload who or what was trying to impede his progress. Kero was truly one of the Lord's more worried creatures.

I didn't have much to do with Kero until several months after Amos had got him. I had occasionally seen Amos work him from the ground and the fence. I'd even caught him riding Kero in the round yard a couple of times. As I had come to expect from any horse that was under the guidance of Amos or Walt, things were going pretty well and I didn't see any sign of real trouble bubbly through Kero. But something about him told me that he was one for the experts and kiddies should not try riding him at home without adult supervision.

I heard the phone ring, but didn't take much notice since it was sure to be some hormonal girl wanting to talk to my older brother. Mum called out, "Ross, phone for you. Amos I think."

"Amos, yeah what's going on?"

"Matey, I want ya to do me a favour. I've got to go into hospital to have a blob taken off me back and I'll be sorta out of action for a couple of weeks. Could ya spend a bit of time with Kero. He's goin real nice and just needs to be ridden kinda quiet. Walt will be around to help ya out if ya need it."

I couldn't say no, but I wanted to. Normally, being asked to ride a horse for Amos or Walt was a great honour - like being asked for a dance by the prettiest girl in school. But the thought of getting on Kero had the same appeal to me as the thought of getting into the boxing ring with Lionel Rose (who was world champion at the time). Kero scared me. I don't know why, but he did.

A couple of days passed and I finally got my courage up. I decide to get Kero out of his paddock and try him out in the round yard. We did a little ground work and I was surprised how soft and easy going this supposedly hot horse seemed to be taking everything. Soon I got him saddled and hopped on board ready for the 'g-forces' from his acceleration around the yard. But nothing went wrong. I walked him and turned him and stopped him and everything seemed just fine. Kero was a little braced in his turns and he wanted to rush his walk just a little, but nothing to worry about. Since Kero was taking everything in his stride, I got off to open the gate and take him into the large arena. Again, he walked, turned and stopped just like in the round yard. Everything was going great. That is until I asked for the trot. Now it became clear why he was called Kero. He was trotting like there was a charging bull behind him. I pulled him up as he tried to fling his head. He stopped going forward, but his feet were still trotting on the spot. It took me ages to get him to walk again. When Kero settled, I tried to trot again. This time he took off in a flat bolt around the arena. There was nothing to do except to turn him into a large circle and gradually wind the circle smaller as he slowed his feet down. Eventually, I got him to a stop and got off, a bit out of breath. I knew I was in trouble here and went looking for Walt.

"Walt, I don't know if I can explain it, but Kero is going great until I try to put a little hurry-up in him. As soon as I ask him to get a bit of life and move it along, he gets terribly upset and overdoes it. What do you reckon is going on with him?"

"Well matey, I ain't seen ya ride Kero today, but I know he's got quite a go button in him. As Amos would tell ya, he is tryin to stay ahead of the pressure. He ain't with ya when the pressure comes on. He's out ahead of ya trying to avoid dealing with the pressure. Ya wanna think about keepin him with ya and you keepin with him. When ya askin for him to hurry up, instead of tryin to make it happen, ya want'a think about lettin it happen. If ya had ever watched him when Amos was riding Kero you'd have maybe noticed that almost nothin happen to get Kero to go softly. That's 'cause Amos would just give Kero the thought to trot and then let it happen."

I wasn't sure what Walt was saying, which wasn't unusual. Thankfully, Walt was used to me asking him to explain himself because there was a lot of stuff that Walt tried to tell me that I didn't understand. I asked him what he meant by 'letting it happen' and 'keeping with him'.

"When ya ask him to trot, cut it by half what ya doin. If he still wantin to be ahead of ya, cut it in half again. Don't be tryin to make it happen by demandin it of him. Keep cuttin it down until it seems like ya askin with nothin. That way he'll learn to stay with ya instead of gettin out there ahead of ya all flustered and worryin. There'll be a spot in there when Kero will think about trottin. At that second ya get out of his way and let it happen. Don't be tryin to get a trot when you want a trot. For now, just add some energy to ya self and let him come up with the idea himself, then let it happen. At that moment you and him will be together. It'll be a beautiful feelin."

It took awhile for Walt's words to sink in. I was used to telling a horse what I wanted and then expecting a result. But Kero was different from most horses I had ridden. He was far more sensitive and worried about being asked to do stuff than any horse I had experienced before. What Walt was trying to tell me was to let Kero find the trot, rather than have me tell him when and how to trot. Kero panicked when a rider asked him to get some life in his feet. Walt was teaching me that if getting life in his feet was Kero's idea, then he was less likely to panic. But Walt didn't tell me how I was going to progress from there to where I could put pressure on Kero and he'd respond just right. I had to ask.

"Well matey, when he gets the feelin of you and him being together and going the same place at the same speed and life is good, he'll get to likin that feelin. It'll be real comfortin to him. Eventually, it'll feel good enough to him that he'll be lookin for it more and more. Soon enough when ya say 'let's go', he'll be right there with ya and be happy to do so. He won't be feelin the need to leave ahead of ya and get bothered. You'll be offerin him somethin he'll be wantin - comfort. A happy horse is a horse that's happy to be with ya, whether on the ground or in the saddle."

Walt was right. In the days ahead I worked at almost doing nothing on Kero. At first I was missing most of the moments when Kero felt he could get some life in his feet, but with Walt's help I began to feel those moments. Soon I was able to let the trot happen and I'd be there right with Kero and we'd be trotting around together as relaxed as you could hope. For a little while they were no more than a few strides, but soon they became laps. And those moments of togetherness grew to seconds and minutes. When Amos got out of hospital he was so pleased with our progress that he allowed me to continue to work with Kero. I was ecstatic that Walt and Amos were there the day that I asked Kero to trot and he was right there with me and was happy to do so. I even suspect that Walt was a touch misty eyed when he came over to tell me I should have more slack in the reins.

From then on, more and more I began looking for those happy horses - the ones that liked to be with a person whether on the ground or in the saddle. They are not as common as you might like to think, but when you have one, you never want to ride an unhappy one again.

DIFFERENT,
BUT THE SAME

It seems at the moment that the rage in horses is Clydesdale crosses. In my business as a trainer I see mostly Warmbloods, Thoroughbreds, Arabs, Quarter Horses and a smattering of other breeds including Clydie crosses. But in the last few months I have been sent more Clydie cross horses than I might normally see in two or three years. I don't know if it is just a coincidence or there has been a sudden surge of popularity in this type of horse.

What has been common about these horses is that almost all the owners have said they bought a Clydie cross because they like the quiet temperament. A few of the owners have ridden some pretty hot horses in the past and turned to the draught bloodlines in the hope of having a nice, easy going and quiet riding horse. While I think that is a perfectly good reason for buying a horse, I sometimes think that people mistake the quiet nature of some horses (of any breed) with easy going. I too believed that to be true until I experienced Walt and Amos at work with two very different, yet not so different horses.

The old brothers had picked up a couple of horses from the market for little more than a song with the idea of working them for a few weeks and then selling them on to help fund repairs to their old Ford truck. Amos had bought Mel – an eight year old Arab mare. And Walt had purchased Boots which was a two year old Percheron gelding with hardly any handling.

It was clear from the beginning that Amos had his hands full with Mel. She was an emu. I mean she would shut down and do nothing until she blasted into hyperdrive and take off. It was all or nothing with her – freeze or warp speed. Boy what a messed up horse she was.

Boots on the other hand was a hoot. I remember the first time I went into his paddock to clean. He had only arrived the day before. He came sniffing around me and the barrow. He was totally fascinated by the smell of the manure of other horses. I tried to shoo him away and he would just stand and look at me, as if to ask what my problem was? He was so easy going. Nothing seemed to bother him. At feeding time he would try to crowd me a little when I walked into his paddock. To keep him away I would swing the bucket at him really violently and even hit him on the shoulder a couple of times, but he didn't seem to register that he wasn't wanted. It seemed to me that he would make a really steady and easy going horse.

Over the next few weeks I watched the old men work their horses. Walt was discovering just how stoic Boots could be. He led like a broken down Sherman tank and needed to be dragged everywhere he went. The pushiness was an ongoing problem. He was so laid back that even getting violent with the flag or a whip was not enough to worry him into keeping his distance from you. He would just trundle along at his half mile and hour speed with a dopey expression and if anything was in his path he would just plough right through. I can't tell you how many times he zapped himself on the electric fence in his paddock in an attempt to stretch his neck for a pick on the other side. I started to call him V.I. which was short for village idiot. But he was cute and was surely going to make somebody a nice riding horse one day. Walt was working Boots from his horse Burner because Burner was the only one strong enough to hold Boots if he tried to leave or if he refused to come forward. It might have taken Walt and Burner three or four days before Boots came around and began to be consistently forward off the lead rope and hardly any drag. Walt would start to ask Boots to come forward and Boots would start to prepare to come forward. It was a very nice change. However, the pushiness took even longer to get a reliable change. Walt worked on keeping him away during feeding every day for nearly two weeks. Each day Boots would try to crowd Walt when he had the feed bucket in his hand and each day Walt would drive him away. Eventually, Boots began to think twice about trying to invade Walt's space. Instead of just walking up to Walt, he began to edge his way forward and it took less and less effort on Walt's part to get Boots to back off. After a couple of weeks, when Walt entered the paddock with a bucket Boots would keep a very respectful distance and follow Walt over to the feeder. He would wait until Walt had emptied the bucket and walked away from the feeder before strolling up to eat his dinner. Boots was getting closer and closer to being a nice horse to be around and I knew Walt would be thinking of breaking him in shortly.

In contrast to the slow progress of Boots, Amos was making real changes to Mel. Within a few days, instead of jumping out of her skin at every little thing, she would register there was a problem then focus her attention on Amos as if she was looking to him for a solution to the trouble. Amos also began to make changes in the way Mel took flight too. He worked her from his riding horse, Billy so that every time Mel tried to leave in a hurry Amos would dally the lead rope to the horn of Billy's saddle and shut her down. If Mel was approaching panic stations, Amos would let the rope slide around the horn to give Mel more freedom to move her feet and not feel so confined, yet still control the situation with Billy's help. A few times Mel tried to attack Billy and Amos out of frustration. She would lunge at them from several feet away or she would try to cow kick at them and a couple of times I saw her nearly bite a hole in Amos' leg. Billy took care of things and kept Amos safe. He never tried to retaliate against the mare, but he kept her positioned just right so that all her threats came to nothing. It was a very impressive demonstration of what could be done with a good horse and a good horseman. The improvements in Mel were almost daily. When Amos began riding her she was tense, but she clearly looked to him for help. One thing you could say about Mel was that she was easy to read because every thought, every emotion was right at the surface for every body to see.

Amos and I talked about what a mess the little mare was in and how bad she must feel inside to be so reactive.

"Yeah matey, she sure came in a pitiful state of mind. Can't possibly know how bad a horse must feel to think that every little thing is going to kill ya," Amos said.

"She is so different from Boots, Amos. Nothing seems to bother him. I reckon you could set a bomb under him and he's probably just think somebody farted," I observed.

"Ya really think they are so different, do ya?

"Well Amos you only have to see how reactive Mel is and how little Boots cares about anything to know they didn't come out of the same mare."

"I think matey, that if ya look below the surface ya might see that they ain't so different."

"How so, Amos" I asked?

"Well, Mel wears her heart on her sleeve. Everythin is there for all the world to see. She don't hide nothin. What ya see is what ya get. But that little Percheron does just the opposite. He stuffs his worries inside. And he's got plenty of worry. He drags around and runs into ya because he don't want to register that ya even there. He figures that if he ignores the world the world will ignore him. So he shuts the world and all its pressure out. He worries about it, but he deals with by pretendin it ain't there. That's how he escapes from it. Mel worries about it too, but she gets all fizzed and flighty and tries to run from it. She figures if she runs fast enough and far enough she'll out run the world and its pressures. Both horses have the same trouble inside them, they just deal with it different-ly. So don't be fooled that Boots is easy goin and don't care too much. He cares plenty, he's just can't deal with it and tries to ignore it. If Walt don't take care and teach Boots to express himself and try to stay tuned into Walt, one day that little fella is goin to pop in a pretty big way. Horses like him can only stuff so much inside themselves before they have to ex-plode. So just because he seems to be quiet don't mean he ain't got trouble inside him. It ain't no different than the trouble in Mel, it's just shows up in a different way and needs to be handled in a different way. But it's the same – just different."

"Well Amos, which is easier to get along with; a horse like Mel or a horse like Boots," I asked?

"Well matey, it depends on what ya more comfortable dealin with.

But one thing I know is that it's often the thing we like most about a horse that gives us the most trouble."

"How do you mean?"

"Matey, people sometimes like a horse that is quiet and don't over react to things. They feel safe on that type of horse. A horse like Boots for instance! But good luck tryin to get that horse to be soft and responsive. Most of them horses are quiet 'cause they don't care or are stuffin stuff deep down inside. Just ask Walt how easy it is to get them horses to be listen softly to the legs and reins. You wait until Walt starts ridin that young fella and see how hard Walt will be workin to get him to go. And when he finally does go, wait and see how hard he is to stop. It's goin to be a project and a half to get that Percheron to be responsive to the rider.

On the other hand, them more sensitive horses, like Mel, are pretty quick to get soft to the reins and legs and it ain't so hard to build a try in them. Lots of people like that in a horse. But those same horses also have a hair trigger and it can be pretty unnervin for some folk when that trigger goes off. So as I said, sometimes the thing we like most in a horse is the thing that gives us sleepless nights."

The story about Boots is not meant to put any one off from buying a nice quiet draught type. The best horse I ever owned was a quiet Percheron gelding that was a lot like Boots to begin with. But it is a warning for folks not to make too many assumptions that a horse that is quiet is also easy going. There may be more trouble than you know brewing inside. But hopefully not.

BEFORE IT HAPPENS

I rode up to see what was keeping Walt. We had made plans to go out for a ride together. Walt was starting a young horse that he was breaking in for a lady and he was ready to take him out for his first trail ride. I was riding Walt's old horse, Burner. I always enjoyed Burner because despite his wonderful education he always made you work. Burner was not an easy horse to ride and it was only Walt that made him look so easy going. I learned something from Burner every time I rode and I rarely turned down a chance to spend time with him.

When I got Burner saddled I rode over to the yards to see what was keeping Walt. I had made arrangements to help Beth (a new girl at the riding school) with worm pasting her horse and didn't want to hang about too long. Walt was still fussing with getting the young horse, Calico, saddled. He hadn't even started any ground work yet, which I knew he would want to do before we rode out! I felt exasperated knowing this was going to take forever and Beth would probably not be in the best of moods for keeping her waiting. This was important to me because I wanted to ask her out to a movie. So I wished Walt would get a hurry along.

"Do you want a hand, Walt," I asked with a smirk (hoping I'd be able to hurry him up)?

"You just don't mind me, matey. Ya gotta enough to worry about with that magnificent steed ya got there to teach ya a bit of humility. He don't like smart alec youngsters."

I sat on Burner and watched and waited while Walt fussed with adjusting the saddle on Calico. He checked the stirrup position on his old stock saddle and stroked Calico under the neck. He shook the back of the saddle, then reached down and gently scratched his hock which caused Calico to lift his left hind leg.

"What the hell is he doing? " I thought to myself.

Walt carried on as if he had all the time in the world to fill in. He reached down for the girth, stopped halfway and stroked Calico again on the shoulder. He then carried on with reaching for the girth. When he got it in his hand he straightened up, then asked Calico to step a front foot back by pressing on his chest. I wondered why he was fussing so much. Eventually, Walt got Calico's girth snugged up. Then he went to reach for the surcingle. Just as he did, he suddenly stopped and stepped backwards two paces. Calico turned his head to Walt and followed him one step. Walt stroked him on the forehead and then reached again for the surcingle. Calico stood quietly as Walt buckled it tight.

I was getting pretty impatient with all this fussing. I knew Calico was fine to saddle and I didn't know or care why Walt was being so slow. My focus was on seeing Beth in a little while and I didn't want to keep her waiting. I was nervous enough about asking her out and didn't need the added aggravation of being late.

Eventually, Walt and Calico were ready. The horse was saddled, bridled and Walt had done enough ground work to satisfy him that all should be well for the short trail ride. The ride was fairly uneventful which is how I guess Walt wanted it to be. Calico was pretty interested in everything he saw, but he walked, trotted and halted all very nicely and without much trouble. I think Walt was quite pleased with the way Calico was handling the situation considering what a nervy and sensitive horse he could be.

We got back to the riding school. I hurriedly unsaddled Burner, gave him a quick brush and trotted him in hand back to his paddock while I left Walt to take care of Calico.

When I got to where Beth was waiting with her horse, Tory, I was out of breath – but I think that had more to do with the way she looked than the fact that I had been running. Beth had told me that her mare was really difficult to worm paste. Tory knew every trick in the book. I was keen to make it look easy to impress Beth and give myself every chance that she would go to a movie with me.

Beth gave me the lead rope and worm paste. I started by just rubbing Tory on the face and working towards her mouth with my free hand. I rubbed around her muzzle and nostrils and then tried to put my thumb in the corner of Tory's mouth. The mare threw her head up high out of my reach and ran backwards. I approached her again and repeated the process. Again Tory was too fast and too strong for me. This went on for several more attempts until I realized I was going to have to try something else. I grabbed her muzzle to distract her while I tried to get the wormer into her mouth. But the horse knew this trick, too. This time she pushed forward and knocked me to the side with her shoulder. Again I had to let go. I knew this wasn't the sort of thing that would impress Beth and my frustration was starting to show. I tried to bring her head around sharply to the left to get some control of her, but she just used her strength to push through me again. This was not going at all according to plan. Over and over I tried what I knew, but every time Tory was a step ahead of me. Not only that, but Tory was losing her patience and she was starting to sweat with anxiety. After awhile I was beginning to think I should give up. It was just then that Walt walked past.

"You two got that horse wormed yet," he asked?

"Not yet, but almost," I replied knowing it was a lie.

"I was wonderin matey, if ya might let me try what ya was showin me the other week? That's if ya young lady don't mind," Walt asked.

"Um, what was I showing you, Walt?" I replied, without a clue to what he was talking about.

"Ya know matey. Ya was showin me how ya a fellow might help get a horse steady by not waitin for a horse to get it wrong, but to give him the right answer before he gives ya the wrong answer."

He turned to Beth and grinned. "I tell ya girlie, I never thought about it much like that before until this young fellow explained it to me. He'll get ya horse wormed in a jiffy, but I wouldn't mind havin a go meself for the practice if ya don't mind," Walt said to Beth.

"Ok. Yeah sure," Beth said looking totally confused. She didn't know Walt at all and was a little unsure about letting this grizzled old guy handle her horse. But she agreed anyway. I didn't know what Walt was going to do or what he was even talking about, but I knew he was trying to help, so I stood back and watched.

Walt took the wormer and the lead rope. He stroked the horse all over and then walked away from the horse. He asked the horse to follow him by stepping Tory's hindquarters away from him. Walt asked Tory to follow him to the left, then the right and left again, and she responded, pretty soft and willing. Then Walt asked for some back ups. Tory would raise her head and shuffle back. Walt worked a little while to get the back ups softer with a lower head position.

After a little while, Walt tried to get his thumb in the corner of Tory's mouth. The horse threw her head up, but before Tory could back away, Walt walked to the side to draw Tory towards him. The horse immediately lowered her head. Then Walt approached Tory's mouth again with his hand, but before Tory could throw her head up, Walt stepped to the side to draw her across. Tory never raised her head. Walt repeated this a few times until he was able to get his thumb in Tory's mouth. Once that was accomplished with little fuss it was a simple process to get the paste tube into the horse's mouth and get her wormed. I doubt the whole think took more than about 7 or 8 minutes. Beth seemed very pleased with how calm Tory took the worm paste even if she didn't know why she was so good.

"How'd I do, matey," asked Walt?

"Um, oh fine Walt. Just fine," I said, a little tongue-tied.

"Thanks matey. Well, I had better go see if Amos has eaten me sandwich. Ya can't trust him when there's food 'round. Thank ya, girlie, that's a nice mare ya got", he said as he handed Beth the lead rope and left to find Amos.

I know that Beth knew that I stuffed up and Walt arrived just in time to save the day. She knew I knew, too. But she went to the movies with me anyway.

Sometime later I found Walt to talk to him about what he had done.

"Well matey, I done the same thing I done with Calico when ya was gettin all upset about how long I took to saddlin. I saw there was trouble inside them horses and I tried to fix it before they needed to take care of it themselves," he answered.

Walt knew I didn't understand and needed further explanation.

"Calico was strugglin with bein saddled. Every time I went to do somethin with the saddle he was thinkin and gettin ready to move. So I helped him by interruptin them thoughts by either rubbin him or movin him before he moved. I tried to fix it before it happened. I did the same thing for that horse with the wormin. She had a habit of throwin her head and runnin back. I was late the first time, but I caught it every other time and got her to change her thought before she moved her feet."

"Ya see matey, everythin a horse does starts with a thought. If ya can see the thought and change it before it becomes an action ya'll never get into trouble. But if ya wait until the thought becomes an action - one ya don't like – ya is always playin catch up with a horse. The later ya are, the stronger the horse's thoughts are and the stronger ya have to be to change them. If ya fix it before it happens, the less ya have to do."

Fix it before it happens? When Walt said that, I remember thinking that I'd have to develop psychic abilities in order to see what the horse was thinking so I could fix it before it happened. But this isn't true. It's really only a matter of awareness of every little thing. I was recently riding on a trail with a small group of people. One lady in particular had a horse that was mentally all over the place. But she didn't notice until he would shy at something. She had to walk home because her horse was too fidgety for her. Another lady was riding a horse that was just as sensitive, but she had a good ride because she was always taking care of things rather than just being a passenger and talking to her friends. Her horse got better as the ride went along, not worse like the other horse. It's all there to read if we stay focused on our horse.

TRAINING WITH INTENT

One of the things that interest me as a trainer and student of horse behaviour is in regard to how a horse understands what we want. I am always impressed at how so many of our horses fill in the gaps in the way we ask. It's as if they already know the answer before the question is completed.

I met a girl called Sarah while I was working at the riding school. Sarah was fifteen years old and only a year older than me. The moment I met her I knew something was not quite normal about her. Sarah was my first experience of some one with cerebral palsy. A few years beforehand Sarah's mum got her interested in horses as a sort of physical therapy. Sarah developed an immediate love of horses and soon had her own horse called Bonny.

Bonny was a great little mare and was always so patient and kind with Sarah's awkwardness. Every weekend Sarah's mum would bring her down to the riding school to ride Bonny. She would haul out a light weight ramp from her van for Sarah to walk up while Bonny led along side and waited for Sarah to get herself organized to get on. It was really something to see and Sarah became one of the most popular kids around the place. Even the cool girls would talk to her. But what most interested me was how Bonny was so good under saddle.

Sarah was always having little spasms. Her muscles would spontaneously contract every few minutes. It would cause her left arm to curl, her neck would twist and when riding her legs would jerk backwards. Yet Bonny never reacted to these spasms. She would carry on with her job just as if Sarah was the quietest rider you could imagine possible. But that is not to say that Bonny was a dull horse - just the opposite in fact. Sarah could ask with hardly any movement and that little mare was right on the job. Her canter transitions were smooth. Her response to the reins was light and her focus on the task was unwavering. Bonny was a very well trained, nice horse and she and Sarah clearly had great communication between them.

But I was intrigued how such a responsive horse could still ignore Sarah's lapse of muscle control. How could Bonny be so responsive to the lightest leg aid or touch of the reins, yet be so unresponsive to Sarah's spasms? I mentioned this to Amos one day when we were watching Sarah riding in the arena.

"Well matey, that mare knows when Sarah is talking to her and when she ain't. That's all."

"But Amos, how can she know the difference," I asked?

"Matey, when I was a kid my grandad got Parkinson disease. That's a sickness where ya nerves act all haywire and ya hands shake, ya voice is slurred and ya ain't got a whole lot of control over ya muscles. A bit like Walt is – only he ain't got Parkinson's disease. Well grandad was a pretty handy horseman in his day. By the time he was in his seventies that disease had a pretty good hold on him and he was not very strong. I remember seein him workin a young geldin not long before he died. He could hardly stand and was leanin on a stick with the lead rope in one hand.

His hand shook so bad that the lead rope looked like it was doin the jitterbug. I watched grandad tell the horse to back up by shakin the lead rope. The only trouble was that I couldn't tell when he was shakin the rope to tell the horse to move or he was just shakin because of the sickness. But ya know what matey, that horse knew. He stepped back when grandad asked as pretty as you could wish. Grandad then asked him to circle around him one way then the other. All I could see was a whole lot of shakin and movin of the rope that didn't have any sense to it. But that geldin did exactly as grandad asked with no fuss or confusion. And it weren't no different when grandad rode the horse. Through all that activity of grandad's shakin and tremours that horse could shift through what had meanin and what didn't.

It ain't no different with young Sarah and her mare. Sarah ain't the prettiest rider. She falls all over the saddle and her limbs can't stay still for more than a few seconds. But that horse has worked out the difference between Sarah's movement that she needs to listen to and the Sarah's movement that she needs to ignore."

"But Amos, how can a horse do that? What tells the horse what is important and what isn't"

"Well matey, it is ya intent."

"What do you mean intent, Amos," I asked?

"Ya seen me ride my horse Cracker with a flag, ain't ya," he asked?

""Yep," I replied.

"And ya seen me ride Cracker while I've been flaggin another horse around the round yard, ain't ya?"

"Yeah," I again responded.

"Well, how do ya expect Cracker knew the difference between when I was talkin to him with the flag and when I was talkin to the other horse? It was me intent. It was the way I focused me and the flag. It's the same for Sarah and Bonny and the same for grandad. A horse can separate ya intent by the way ya focus ya use of ya reins, ya legs or ya body."

"Amos, are horses really clever enough to do that," I asked sceptically?

"Matey, not only are they good at it, they are better at it than you or I. Ya don't believe me do ya? Have ya ever spoken to somebody on the phone and they answered all ya questions, but ya had a feelin they were distracted or had somethin else on their mind? That you was more involved in the conversation that they were. Ya couldn't see what they were doin or what they were lookin at, but ya knew that there focus was some where else. It's the same thing with a horse. They know when ya mean it and they know when ya don't.

Like most of my experiences with Walt and Amos, the conversation I had just had didn't have a lot of meaning to me at the time. I found Amos' observations interesting and kept looking for evidence of his theory. There is no doubt in my mind that he was right. Horses can discern intent. I have seen it enough times when two people use the same technique on the same horse and get different results. Horses know the difference of our intent.

It is also been my observation that some of the most effective horse riders have been people who have less than perfect technique. Most of us spend a lifetime learning to become better riders and for most of us this means riding in the perfect position and using the perfect aids with perfect timing. Yet, so many riders with good position and good technique have screwed up horses. Why is this? I believe it is because nobody is teaching the effectiveness of "intent". Consistency and intent beat technique and position every time. A horse can rise above the obstacle of a rider with less than perfect balance or understanding of the aids, if the rider is clear in what they are trying to achieve.

I am not suggesting for one second that learning to sit and ride better is not important and a worthy goal, but I am suggesting that it is secondary to being consistent and clear in your intent. Sarah and Amos' grandad proved that.

GIVE A HORSE A CHANCE

A few months back I was at a dinner party with some friends. A couple of them were close friends and some were just friends of friends whom I knew from occasional get-togethers. All the women were horsey. So, much to the chagrin of their husbands at the table, the conversation naturally turned to horses. Because everybody knew that I was a trainer, a lot of the conversation seemed directed to me. I was told about the trials, tribulations and success of each person's horse. It was as if each one was looking to me for approval for what they had done or not done with their horses. I felt like the psychiatrist at a party where everybody wanted me to confirm that they were not nuts.

At one point I was talking with a lady who liked to compete in show classes. She had only had her horse about 6 months and said he was trouble-free except he pig rooted in the canter transitions. That was his only problem according to her. She admitted that the horse had gone really well in the first few weeks and she really loved him. But since the horse developed the pig rooting problem she was beginning to think she had made a mistake. She said she was getting help from a local coach. The coach had told her that she should give the horse another couple of months of work. If the horse didn't make the grade by then she should sell him. After all, what good is a show horse that pig roots?

The lady droned on and on and my mind stopped listening. Instead I started to wonder, why does somebody like this have a horse? It has always bamboozled me how somebody can claim to love their horses with so much passion when things are going well. But in a matter of days or weeks decide to sell a horse because they have hit a hiccup in the work. Was it because people wanted their relationship with their horse to be problem free? I guess it is understandable in the light that most people can't have a problem-free life in their dealings with people. Maybe they go looking for it in their relationship with their animals. Or perhaps people like horses to pamper their ego. If your horse is working well, it feels good. Others admire your horse, judges reward you for your work with your horse and you become recognized as being good with horses. But if your horse does not go well it is hard to find much to boost your ego or your confidence.

I was reminded of a time when Amos was driving me across Sydney to a show. He was driving the old beat up Bedford truck and we had Hank in the back. Hank was a 16.1hh thoroughbred that I had been jumping at shows around Sydney. Hank's owner was our usual means of transport, but she had a family day and was not able to come along. Amos was kind enough to volunteer to act as driver, groom and coach.

We had been talking away for awhile. Well actually I had been trying to pump him for information about his past. Amos and his twin Walt seemed to have no past. They never talked about much except horses and I wanted to know more about them. But Amos was a pretty cool customer and evaded most of my questions with his own questions. At one point he asked me which was my favourite horse at the moment.

"Hank!" I said.

"Why?"

"Well, because he wins nearly everything we enter. I reckon we will be in B grade before the end of the season," I replied.

Amos was quiet in thought for a few moments. I thought it was just because he was waiting for the traffic light to change green. Then he said, "See them two fellows over there with them whipper snippers cuttin the grass on that bank?"

"Yeah."

"Which one would you give a job," he asked?

I watched for a little while. I thought Amos was trying to give me a trick question. It was obvious that the fellow in the blue shirt had done more grass cutting on his side of the bank. He also seemed to have done a smoother job. The fellow in the hat had missed a few spots and would have to go back to cut the grass more evenly.

I said, "I'd give the fellow in the blue shirt a job first."

"Why," Amos asked?

"Because he seems to be a harder worker and has done a better job," I said with some confidence.

"What if I told ya the fellow with the hat is tryin just as hard or maybe harder than the other fellow, but he just wasn't as talented at cuttin grass?" Amos threw in.

"Well, if I was paying them I'd still want the guy who was going to do the better job," was my reply.

"Well then matey, who looks after the other fellow," Amos asked?

"What do you mean, Amos?"

"Well matey, the bloke in the blue shirt is a good worker. No doubt. In fact, so good that he'll get a job anywhere. He'd have no trouble getting a job. He'll always be able to look after himself, feed his family and pay his bills. But the fellow in the hat probably won't be able to always get a job when there are fellows with blue shirts to take those jobs. So who looks after him? Who feeds his family and pay his bills? He's doin the best he can, but he just can't compete with fellows in blue shirts when it comes to cuttin grass."

"So, would you give the fellow in the hat a job, Amos?"

"Maybe. Maybe I can help a fellow like that. Maybe I can teach him to try harder or teach him a skill that he'd be better at than cuttin grass or maybe I can just help him find the fun in his work. I dunno that I can do any of those things or that it would even be a smart thing to give him a job. But maybe it'd be the smartest thing I ever did 'cause he'd maybe turn out to be the best worker I ever had. But at least I know I had done somethin for him and his family. Because I gave him a job when he needed it and nobody else would."

I was confused. I knew Amos had a message in there for me, but I couldn't get it.

"What are you talking about, Amos?"

"Matey, a relationship can be many things. But the best relationships are never one sided. You'd give the fellow in the blue shirt a job because you reckon he'd work for you better than the other fellow. You think Hank is the best horse you've ridden in quite awhile because he wins more ribbons for you. What do you give back to Hank? Nothin. Nothin that you don't give to those other horses. Would you still like Hank just as much if he still tried as hard, but never won anythin?

"You like things because it's about what you get back. When you find a relationship that you have to put in as much as you get back, you'll know what I mean. The best relationships you'll ever have will be the ones when you can contribute. That goes for your horses, your dogs, your friends and for anybody you give a job."

I think I now know what Amos was talking about. Over the years I think the horses I have most enjoyed are the ones who were the most in trouble and for whom I was able to give the most help. None of those horses ever became more than safe to ride. None achieved success at higher levels of competition - none of them had enough talent. But they were able to find a spot in their life where they could get along with humans and do the best they could every time somebody asked something of them. The lesson Amos taught me was to enjoy horses for what they are and not for what I wanted them to be.

ONE STEP BACKWARD, TWO STEPS FORWARD

Ever since Walt and Amos had me under their mutual wing as a de facto apprentice horseman, a few people had started to seek my opinion on problems they had been having with their horses. At first I was taken aback at the thought that anybody would want my views and then even horrified that they actually listened and put them into practice. I couldn't understand why they would ask me when Walt or Amos visited the riding school nearly everyday. After all, these old brothers had accumulated more years around horses than I was ever likely to achieve. They knew so much more about horses than anybody else that I had known. They were gentle with horses and seemed to understand what was inside a horse before it ever got to the outside. But I later discovered that many people thought they were a bit eccentric and it was often difficult to interpret their meaning when they told you something. Both fellows had a way of talking in obscurities and leaving you to work out the meaning. I guess this is why people started approaching me with their questions. By this stage I had learned the language of the old men and could turn their words into plain English.

Terry had been a boarder at the riding school for a few months. He was a teacher of ancient history which explains why he called his horse Plutarch. Terry came to me one day while I was cleaning stables and asked if I had any advice about a problem Plutarch had developed over recent weeks. He said that if they went on a trail ride, Plutarch would go only so far down the road and then stop and start backing up. At first the horse would only back up a bit. But it was getting worse and he was now backing up quickly and a long way with no regard to what he might run into behind him. I told Terry that maybe I should take Plutarch for a ride and see for myself. He agreed and we made a time for the next week.

Plutarch was a pretty steady horse. He had a good walk and although he looked around a lot, he wasn't walking with one foot on the brake. We got down the road a bit and turned the corner to head up onto a bush track. Plutarch just stopped. At first I thought he was afraid to step onto the embankment, but I quickly realized that this was part of his pattern. I asked him to go forward with a little leg and he immediately raised his head and started in reverse gear. He shook his head with every step. I applied more leg but this seemed to get him going backwards faster. I cracked him with a whack of my hand on his rump as hard as possible, but was rewarded with a buck followed by a back up at full speed. The only thing that stopped us was a tree that he hit with his rear end. He then jumped forward one stride, reared and began to run backwards around the tree so fast that he fell on his hocks. I managed to stay on. At this point, horse and I were a bit shaken and we both stood there wondering what to do next. I remembered reading that a horse must always go forward in response to leg aids. This was a maxim of dressage - not to be questioned! So I kicked Plutarch again and again. He started backing up quickly not seeming to care where he was going or what he might run into.

I felt it was time to change strategy again. I figured that if he wanted to back up so much I would encourage him to back up until he got so sick and tired of backing that forward would seem a really good idea. I asked him to back and back and back. We had backed up over a hundred meters before Plutarch got stuck and decided backing was too hard. I then squeezed with my legs to ask him to go forward, but he just started backing again. I encouraged him to keep backing with the reins. After some distance he stopped backing and again I asked for forward. This time he reared up. I tried backing him again, but he reared. I tried asking for forward, but he reared. I was really in a bind here. After 20 minutes of trying everything I knew to get this horse to go forward I gave up and headed home. Plutarch didn't give me one ounce of trouble on the trip home and I knew that he knew something that I didn't know.

I was at a loss what to tell Terry because my skills fell short for a problem like this. I knew it was time to call in the big guns. I went in search of Walt and Amos. I found them both washing the sticky paspalum grass off their horse's legs and chests. I sat down and watched them a bit when Walt asked me what it is I was wanting. I explained about Terry's horse and what had happened on our ride.

Amos said, "Sometimes ya seem to like to make hard work out of somethin that ought to be simple. Why did ya try to out muscle a beast ten times ya size. You think your puny kicks is goin to change the mind of a horse much bigger than ya when he's made up his mind to get his tail home before his nose. Sometimes I wonder about ya, matey. Tomorrow, same time, be here."

I knew our conversation had ended and I was expected to show up tomorrow for a lesson with Amos.

When I arrived for my lesson with Amos, Terry had Plutarch ready to go.

Amos started with a lecture. "Now matey when Terry's horse starts to back up ya not going to make him go forward. Don't go gettin all macho and try to make it happen. I'll walk along side ya and you listen to what I gotta say real careful."

I rode down the road and Amos and Terry walked a little distance behind. It took about 5 minutes to get to that same spot we had trouble yesterday. Plutarch immediately stopped when I tried to steer him up the embankment and then started to back up. I then heard Amos right beside me. I remember thinking how surprised I was at how much ground Amos had covered in a few seconds because I was sure he was a good way behind a couple of heart beats ago.

"Matey, don't go gettin strong with them legs. Just bump him kinda gently."

Plutarch immediately hollowed out and picked up his pace of backing.

"Too much! Too much! Just a little bump. Keep bumpin just a little. And use ya reins to guide him from runnin into anythin. Now maybe just touch his elbow with ya toe with each bump – just one leg at a time."

Plutarch kept backing up. But at an even pace - not rushing or panicky at all. I steered him around the tree as he reversed and kept him on the track with gentle use of the reins. I realized that he was much more mentally focused than yesterday which made steering easier. He was still going back, but there was no panic about it. We had backed up more than half way home and my legs were getting tired. But Amos kept telling me to bump him gently. Finally, Plutarch stopped going back.

"Stop bumpin matey. Sit there and rub his withers gently for a minute or two. That's good. Now ask him to go forward."

I squeezed with my legs and Plutarch starting backing again. With Amos' encouragement I began bumping him again. This time we must have only gone 40 or 50 meters before he stopped and stood still. I gently rubbed his neck and withers and sat quietly for a few moments. Then I ask for another forward. Again Plutarch began to back. However, with my constant bumping he only went about 6 steps before stopping. After I rubbed him some more and asked him to go he walked about 3 steps forward before stopping and backing up. I kept up the bumping until he again could stop, then go forward when asked. We had traveled in reverse almost to the front gate before Plutarch began to show a change. When I finally got about 20 steps forward without hesitation Amos told me to ask him to stop and to head home.

"Ya don't have to take him on a big trip today. He just needs to learn that goin forward to an ask from ya leg is enough to give him a break. If ya ask for a big ride today ya likely to turn going forward into work and undo all the good stuff ya just done. Let him know that backing up to the leg is what causes the discomfort. Now when ya get home, go into the arena and canter him around for 10 minutes with lots of transitions and lots or change in direction. If ya do that after every ride for awhile he might not be in such a big hurry to get home when ya take him out."

It took a day of thinking about everything that Amos said before I could clarify my thoughts on what I had learned. I was still unsure about why it was that when I tried to kick Plutarch forward things got worse, but when I gently bumped him with my leg things got better. I had to ask Amos.

"Well matey, when Terry's horse started backing up he had his mind on the front gate. Terry had taught him that if he could get near that front gate he'd get unsaddled and put back in his paddock where he could eat and rest. So going out for a ride was not so nearly a good a choice as backin all the way home. Terry's horse is a pretty sensitive gelding and when ya started kicking him he started feelin threatened. Ya put him in a bind and ya turned off his ability to respond with anythin except his instinct for survival. His mind was going backwards, his feet was wantin to go backwards and you came in with all guns blazin and got him tied up in knots."

"And that thing when ya tried to get him tired of backin up by makin him back up more than he wanted was not one of ya best ideas. He was already in trouble and in a mental bind. He didn't know what to do when ya told him he to back. He tried goin back and that gave him no relief from ya reins. His mind was still tellin him to go back, so he wasn't wantin to go forward. The only thing left for him was to go up. Ya gave him no choice. Besides matey, ya never want to get a horse to be sick of goin back. Ya never know when you are likely to need it and if has learned to hate goin back his backup might not be there when ya need it."

"So Amos was the tapping him with my leg meant to put just enough pressure to make backing up uncomfortable, but not enough to get him in a bind," I asked?

"You got it matey. Horses are always lookin for comfort and safety. The bumpin with one leg was enough to say that backin up was not as comfortable as he thought, but not so uncomfortable that he felt he was in trouble. If ya try to force a horse to change his ideas, he'll fight ya with whatever survival tool he has in his kit. But by keepin the pressure below what would trigger his sense of survival, ya just need to wait for the horse to change his mind about what works and what doesn't work for him. See, Terry has taught his horse that backin up works as a way of gettin comfort. Now he needs to re-teach his horse that it doesn't work and that goin forward is the easiest way to comfort. Horses are really dead simple in the way life works for them."

In the following days Terry and I worked together with Plutarch to overcome his habit of backing up when he wanted to head home. We kept up Amos' advice and found it even worked well when we came across obstacles like puddles and bridges. Plutarch got pretty good as a trail horse and I learned a lot about pressure and staying on the right side of trouble to get a job done. I learned that doing less and taking more time was a better deal for the horse and the trainer.

DO YOU OWN A HORSE?

I can expect a phone call about once a month from the secretary of an adult riding club or pony club or jumping club or dressage club or trail club to ask for my services on one of their rally days. I try to attend as many of these as I can and give what help is possible with people's horse problems, given the limited time available.

A few months ago I was running a session at a dressage club for people who were struggling with collection in their horses. Mostly I find there is a problem with peoples understanding as to what collection really means. However, once I pass along the idea, I then try to establish for them the feel in the horse's hindquarters that they need in order to get collection started.

This particular day the session went pretty well and everybody seemed to get a good change in their horses. One lady came up to me after her lesson and thanked me for a breakthrough in her thinking and in her horse. She had been having problems with collection for a long time and discovered that she had been trying to make it happen rather than prepare the horse properly so he can find it himself when the time is right. As people have a tendency to do, she then asked about my background and my horses. When she asked how many horses I owned, I had an immediate flashback to a time so long ago that I could not have been much more than 10 years old.

I had just started to work at the riding school. My job was to clean stables and feed horses. I was working two days a week and in return I got two free riding lessons. There were lots of boarders at the riding school. Mostly they were young girls and middle aged ladies. Of the few men that were regularly hanging around, the most conspicuous were the old men, Walt and Amos.

Being the new kid, I tried to be friendly to everybody. One day I saw Walt working a horse in the arena. I went up and hung off the gate. As he passed by I asked, "Is this a new horse?"

"Yep," was the reply.

In order to keep the conversation going I asked, "Have you got many horses?"

"Nope."

"Well, how many do you own," I tried one more time?

"None. Don't own none," was Walt's reply as he continued to ride past.

I was a bit incredulous because I had seen Walt and Amos work several horses. I asked, "You don't own any horses?"

"Nope."

"But I've seen you ride stacks of horses," I asked further.

Walt stopped for a moment, "Why sure. I ride them horses but I don't own them. I guess I'm just responsible for them. I ain't never owned a horse, but I sure been responsible for a heap of them." He then got on with the job I had interrupted as if he had said everything he needed to say and that was the end of the conversation.

I know I missed Walt's point at the tender age of ten. It took a few years to pass before his words really meant something to me. Walt had paid money for those horses and legally he did own them, but in Walt's eyes he didn't own them. He was just given the job of making sure they had a good life.

Years later Walt told me, "The notion of ownin a horse is like sayin you own a child or you own a wife. There ain't no such thing. But I figure if they come home with me, then I am responsible for them. That don't mean I own them. It just means I gotta take care of them. Same thing holds for a horse. Ain't no different."

Walt then told me I should read a book called the *The Little Prince* by Antoine St Exupery. "Everythin ya need to know about responsibility and carin for a horse is in there."

I discovered *The Little Prince* was a children's book, and couldn't imagine what a kid's book could teach me about horses. It didn't even have a horse in the story, just a kid from outer space, a man, a rose, a fox and a few other weird characters. Eventually, I got around to reading it. It is a very short book, so it didn't take any time at all to finish. After reading it three times, I understood exactly the point Walt was trying to make. I see it on a weekly basis. People get caught up in the idea of owning things. I guess in some ways this is necessary in order to keep legal entitlements of what belongs to whom from becoming chaotic. But it then becomes part of the mind set of the owner. The notion of ownership takes over the ego of the owner.

If a person strives to gain the most out of a relationship with a horse, they need to have a fair degree of humility. One needs to accept that the horse has a great deal to teach us and that nobody knows more about the needs of the horse than the horse. From experience, I can tell you that this is incredibly difficult to achieve. Most people have a very strong sense of superiority when it comes to animals. We believe that we are smarter and we know what's best. It is almost impossible to discard this smugness because it is so vigorously fueled by the notion of owning the animal. If I own an animal, I must be the superior. This is how most of us think whether we admit it or not. I believe when we have this attitude toward our horses we inevitably make it the horses responsibility to obey our wishes. We take the stance that if the horse is not behaving as we wish, then he is being a mongrel with a bad attitude. After all, we buy rugs to keep him warm, we buy expensive saddlery to help him work comfortably, we make sure he doesn't go hungry, we pay a lot to ensure he is healthy. We do all those things, so the least you'd reckon you can expect is for the horse to try to behave as we want.

I've heard so many folk express in some form or other the fact that they spend a lot of money and time and they care so much about their horses that they feel the horse has let them down for not being a good horse to ride. In these instances, I believe the owners are missing an understanding of what their real responsibilities are towards their horse.

When I was a teenager I had a friend called Micky (short for Michelle). Her dad had bought her a very expensive show jumper from South Australia who she called Gumboot. Micky made sure that Gumboot had an array of the warmest and most expensive rugs, the prettiest custom-made tack and saddlery and the best protective gear for the horse. She brushed him every day, pulled his mane and washed him regularly and cleaned his gear after every use. Micky was doing everything she thought she needed in order to do the right thing by her horse. Yet, Micky and her horse didn't get along too well when it came to working together. He was hard to pull up and was constantly throwing his head around on the jump course. If you had hooked up his tail to an electrical generator you could probably have powered a town the size of Tamworth.

One day I passed comment about the trouble that Micky had been having with Trident to Walt.

"Well matey, if she'd put half as much effort into gettin his mind fixed as she does in brushin him, she'd have a pretty good horse," Walt said.

"How do you mean," I asked?

"Micky thinks she is doin the right thing by that horse when she buys them rugs or brushes him every day. Horses don't care about that stuff. That's somethin we humans do to make us feel like we care for our horses. If she really wanted to do the right thing by her horse she'd spend more time and more money in learnin how to understand him. If she really wanted to do somethin for her horse to show how much she cares she could teach him to soften to them reins so she could throw away that big bit and that martingale and that noseband.

"When a person has a horse they have a job to do. Most people think that job is to have them lookin pretty and fed right. But the most important job they have is to make the horse feel good inside himself. Too many people worry about the superficial stuff and that stuff don't mean much to the horse. When ya gotta horse you gotta responsibility to help him feel right about working with ya."

What Walt had to say about responsibility all those years ago echoed in my head as the lady asked me how many horses I owned.

"None," I said. "I've got a couple at home that I'm responsible for and maybe they own me, but I don't own any horses."

I'm not sure my words meant anything to the lady. I tried to convey the notion that having horses in your life is about accepting a responsibility for their well-being on the inside and on the outside - it isn't about ownership and it isn't about what a horse owes us. Walt knew that from the horse's point of view it is much better to spend time and money on learning to understand them than it is to buy a new rug every year.

KEEPING THE HORSE
IN THE HORSE

The thrill of being chosen as a winner was mind numbing stuff. I had been honoured as one of 5 young riders to attend a week long dressage camp with one of the countries pre-eminent coaches on the outskirts of Sydney. It was very exciting because I figured I was now on the verge of learning all the secrets that turned people from good riders to great riders. Walt and Amos had taught me a lot about how a horse thinks and feels, but they had been less helpful when I wanted to learn how to teach a horse to perform passage or piaffe and all those other higher goals of riding. I wondered whether it was something that they didn't really understand themselves. This was an opportunity to absorb the secret mysteries that only the best riders knew.

Unfortunately, I didn't have a horse of my own at the time. In fact, in all the years I had been riding I never owned a horse. Even though I was 15 and had been riding 7 years, I had not been fortunate enough to have a horse for which I was solely responsible. I had always ridden other people's horses. Most often, it was Walt and Amos who allowed me to work a horse, but sometimes I could ride a school horse. However, lately I had been asked more and more by other owners to ride their horses in competition. I guess people liked to see their horses coming home with ribbons that they could proudly display to their friends and family. I had a few regulars who owned some pretty nice show jumpers, but who were a little nervous about competing themselves.

In any case, I didn't have a horse to take to the dressage camp until Amos offered a little buckskin that he had recently broken-in (in those days it was still politically ok to call it breaking-in!). I knew it was a grand gesture on the part of Amos to offer me this horse, but I was also not thrilled by the offer. The other kids would be taking their zillion dollar 16hh horses that had been in training for 700 years and were competing at inter-galactic level. I'd be the joke of the week with a 15hh buckskin that Amos had picked up for a few dollars at the auction and who was greener than a tree frog. I dreaded the thought, but what choice did I have other than to pull out? At least I was able to borrow a dressage saddle and bridle, instead of having to use Amos' old stock saddle and barco bridle.

Walt and Amos offered to drive me and Bucky to what was to be our home for the week. I felt like a teenager whose mother still kissed him at the school gate in front of his mates. But again what choice did I have? It was a long drive across the other side of Sydney and the old truck threatened to boil over a couple of times when we got stuck in city traffic. On arrival the master and his wife greeted us with some apprehension. I think we were a little out of place among the fancy floats and vehicles and the very expensive horses. The first session of lessons was to start in 30 minutes and parents were invited to stay for the morning. I'm ashamed to admit now that I was embarrassed by Walt and Amos. Their appearance, their manner and their style of speech were so different from the others that I felt I didn't want to be associated with them. Walt sensed this and said they wouldn't stay, but Amos insisted on watching how Bucky would do.

As I was saddling I got a chance to watch some of the other kids who had already started warming up in the arena. When everybody was gathered the master asked each of us about ourselves and our horses. All the other horses had years of training. Bucky was only broken in a month before the camp. The master asked us all to walk and trot around so he could assess each of us. I was too nervous to take much notice of anybody else and every time I saw the master looking my way I felt myself stiffen. I really felt out of place and in over my head. I wanted to go home.

After about 10 or 15 minutes we were told to stop and gather in the centre of the arena. The master then looked at me and told me to ride out. I felt sure I was about to be humiliated and sweat exploded from my brow. The master asked me to walk, then trot, halt, trot off, circle right, circle left, canter and rein back. He then thanked me, then turned to the others and said, "Did anyone notice how soft and forward this horse goes? It is obvious to me and it should be obvious to all of you that this little horse enjoys his work and is ready at all times to do something. It is my hope that by the end of the week that we will have every horse here working as softly as Ross' horse."

I was stunned. Bucky wasn't round and collected. Bucky didn't have a nice lather of foam coming out of his mouth. Bucky didn't respond well to a short contact. All these other horses had arched necks and high tails. They had sweat on their chest and down their flanks. They had real presence. They looked like dressage horses. What did he mean that he hoped they were going as well as Bucky by the end of the week?

I looked at Amos whose chest seemed to have expanded beyond the breaking point of his shirt buttons. He was beaming.

I learned a lot that week. But what stands out in my mind is that the master saw in Bucky something that all the other horses lacked. I talked to him about it later. I asked him how come if the other horses could perform flying changes, pirouette and counter canter that he thought Bucky was better trained.

"Bucky is a horse. The others used to be horses," he replied.

"What do you mean?"

"What your friend Amos did for Bucky was allow the horse in him to learn to get along with the rider in you. He showed Bucky that he could still be a horse and at the same time follow a lead. What happens to most horses is they are trained to be slaves. The lose their pizzazz, they lose their essence as horses. It is the essence of a horse that makes most people fall in love with them. The trouble is that we become so focused on teaching a flying change that we train the horse out of the horse and replace him with a simple moving cardboard cutout of a horse doing a flying change."

I thought for a moment and said, "I guess I didn't know you could do that. I've spent so much time around Walt and Amos that I reckon that their way is normal. I didn't want to bring Bucky because I wanted a horse that could do all the fancy maneuvers so I could learn the Grand Prix stuff."

"You have been very fortunate, Ross. Your friends are true horsemen and every horse and every rider should be lucky enough to have friends like that. They have instilled in you and the buckskin the basic skills that make it possible for you to achieve anything you want. And they have allowed you to still be a teenager and your horse to be a horse!"

The folly of being a teenager didn't allow the master's words to really sink in for some time. But when they did I was never again embarrassed about Walt and Amos. The master was right when he said that some people train the horse out of their horses because it is not a horse that they want. Instead they want a push-button slave who performs on command. I doubt it ever occurred to Walt and Amos to train the horse out of a horse.

THE TROUBLE WITH THOROUGHBREDS

Hi name was Dusty. That wasn't his registered racing name, but it was the name he got once Lee bought him. Dusty had raced in NSW for the last three years by a fellow who was a small time owner with a passion for his horses and racing. Dusty's career consisted of one win and several placings at provisional meetings, but he never made it as the city winner that his owner had hoped. Lee managed to buy Dusty through contact with a friend of a friend which is how he ended up being agisted at the riding school at which I worked.

When he first arrived at the riding school he needed quite a lot of feeding and time to settle in. He was quiet and friendly and had clearly been handled with a lot of love in his life. Dusty never gave me trouble at feeding time or when cleaning his stable. I remember telling Walt that I thought he was a nice horse and Walt telling me that Dusty was trying to be a nice horse, but that there was trouble inside of him. I didn't know how Walt could know this because Lee hadn't even begun to work him by this stage. But Walt was no fool, so I took a special interest in Dusty's progress.

The first day of training began with Lee lunging her 16 hh gelding in side reins and a surcingle. There wasn't a lot of finesse or control going on at first. Dusty would walk out on the circle ok, but shortly he offered a trot that got faster and faster. In Lee's desperation to get some control back she pulled the lunge line which caused Dusty to pull away from her and run backwards in a mad flight. After a few strides he stopped running and looked at her with a panicked expression. Lee tried again and Dusty took off in a rush on the circle. This time I think Lee decided to let him run in a circle until he got tired. I didn't get to see too much more of this because duties called.

A few days later I was getting some horses ready for a riding lesson that the boss had booked when I noticed Lee was riding Dusty in the arena. The horse was trotting around the track with his head high and his mouth gaped open. The trot was pretty fast and Lee was trying to slow it down by leaning against the reins. When she asked him to circle it looked more like she was trying to turn a semi-trailer without power steering. After I finished saddling the horses for the lesson, I noticed Lee was riding Dusty down the laneway between the paddocks. She still had a pretty tight hold of those reins and Dusty still looked like he was trying to breath in jet fumes, but both were holding it together. That is until a couple of horses came running alongside the fence line. Dusty started to charge off down the laneway, but Lee managed to get a stronger hold on the reins. Then Dusty gave a half-hearted rear followed by several leaps forward until he got a safe distance from the trotting horses. He finally settled back into a walk, but Lee was clearly rattled and wasn't going to let go of the hold she had on him.

A week or so later I saw Lee riding Dusty again in the arena. It was looking better than the previous episode, but he was still a little rushy and Lee was still riding as if Dusty was about to leave the arena without asking first. Over the next few weeks, Lee continued to work with Dusty and was getting some instruction by a professional coach. I saw the instructor riding Dusty and he had his head down and tucked in. His forward was more controlled, but if anything his stride was half the length it was a couple of weeks before. I asked Lee how Dusty was going.

"Oh, he is going great. I love him so much. My instructor really likes him and thinks he has terrific potential. But he knows he can put one over on me and she is helping me to teach him not to be so piggy. When he doesn't want to do something he can be such a brat. But he is learning that won't work anymore."

Over the next few weeks I kept tabs on Dusty and would check to see if Lee was riding him whenever I was at the riding school. I really liked him and hoped I would get a ride on him one day. Lee worked him mostly in the arena. It was obvious they had their good and bad days just like everybody, but I noticed Lee never took him out the arena anymore.

"Well, I took him out a few times, but he gets so spastic when he is out of the arena. I think he must think he is still at the race track. I was thinking of putting him on some of that herbal calming stuff. A friend of mine uses it and swears by it."

I don't know if she ever did put Dusty on some sort of calming supplement, but she hardly ever took him out of the arena again and things in the arena were about to take a turn for the worse.

Lee had been riding Dusty for a little over two months when he reared on her in the arena. She told me that he had been going really well. She had started using a market harborough on him about two weeks earlier and that seemed to make a big improvement in his response to the reins although he was more fidgety. But on this day after Lee had asked him to canter, Dusty propped his feet and stopped. She said she nudged him forward and he stomped with both front feet and reared. The first rear was only half a rear, but apparently the second rear had Lee looking skyward. She fell off and Dusty took off bucking around the arena for a minute. He finally stopped at the far end when his front foot got caught in the reins. Lee was physically ok, but was pretty shaken. She later talked to me about what had happened and said that it seemed to come from nowhere. She said that he had been getting gradually worse the last couple of weeks and she didn't know what to do. Her instructor thought she needed to be a stronger rider, but she didn't think she could be much stronger. I asked her did she think that introducing the market harborough two weeks ago and his deteriorating behaviour under saddle were related? She said that it helped keep his head down and that made him more responsive to the reins. Her instructor thought things were getting better. I said that if I were her I'd have a talk to Walt or Amos. They understood horses better than anybody else I knew, so maybe they could help her. She agreed and we went looking for Walt.

"Well girlie, I seen some of what Dusty has been gettin up to with ya.

I think I understand his problem, but I don't think ya goin to like it."

"Well, tell me what you think is the problem Walt. I don't know where to go from here and I'm thinking that I might sell him before he either hurts me or scares me too much for me to want to ride again," said Lee.

"Well girlie, the problem is that he ain't broke."

The answer left Lee and I both in shock. What did he mean the horse isn't broken in? Of course he is. Dusty was started as a two year old and ridden for the last three years! Walt obviously saw the disbelief in our faces.

"What I mean girlie is that he ain't broke!" As if repeating himself made it somehow clearer.

"Dusty was broke in to race. Which means he don't buck. He's goes, but don't stop too well. He turns sort of, but he don't get a bend in his body. He don't know what it's like to have a rider that don't hang on his mouth. He don't know what it's like to move without his nerves bein all jittery. He ain't broke!"

Walt looked at us as if we are suppose to have understood all that and it all made sense why Dusty reared and what Lee needs to do to fix the problem. But of course none of that was true. Walt saw our dismay and tried to explain.

"Girlie, ya bought a horse that ya figured was broke. He'd been ridden for so many years and ya figured he was sort of educated in the ways of the world. So ya bring him home and try to teach him dressage. Ya treat him like a horse that might have been broke and ridden for a few years. Ya try to get 'im round. Ya expect 'im to be relaxed and not fussed about so many things. Ya try to get 'im to canter by using ya seat, rein and legs in a way that means nothin to 'im. And that might be ok if he had the education that a ridin horse might get. But he ain't. He don't even know how to stand still so ya can get aboard! All he knew when ya bought 'im was to not buck and go like the clappers when them barrier gates opened up. There's all this stuff that's missing that he should know by now."

"What do I do about it, Walt," Lee asked?

"Well girlie, ya treat 'im like he ain't been broke. Go back to square one and fill in all the gaps that were missed when he was broken in the first time. He's a smart horse. He'll catch on real quick. But ya problem is simple and so common. I see people all the time get horses off the track and start ridin them like they were already ridin horses. Occassionally ya get one that takes to ridin without too much of a hitch. But most don't and lots of them end up gettin sold again and again until somebody either works out that they ain't broke or the doggers pick them up. If ya wanna keep Dusty and teach 'im to be a good ridin horse start today like it is his first day at the breakers. Some stuff you'll find he knows ok and ya move right along with that, but other stuff he won't know or what he knows about it is bad. That stuff ya want to spend some time on gettin right before ya go further. It takes time and patience, but you'll end up with a nice horse in a few months.

Walt's words are still true. People get 'off the track thoroughbreds' and treat them like they have been well educated and ridden since they were two years old. Most horse people realize that racing screws up the minds (and often the bodies) of most young thoroughbreds. But for some reason they still expect that the one they bought should be good to ride and if he isn't it is because he is trying to put one over on them or because he is getting too much lucerne or because he is reliving his racing days. Some of the best horses I have had have been rehabilitated ex-race horses. But I took the time to re-break them and treat them like horses with damaged minds. I was always happy when they gave me good stuff and never surprised by the poor stuff that was brewing inside them.

ENOUGH

I always thought how nice it would be to have a horse of my own and start him from scratch. If I could get a horse that nobody had stuffed up and begin at the beginning, then I just knew it had to be easier than taking a ruined horse and fixing him. I had never said any of this to Walt and Amos, but it was just an idea that seemed so obvious I knew it must be true. The old men had always said that it was easier to fix a problem before it happened than wait until it was a problem. So I was itching to start a young horse with a clean slate. It seemed that this was the only way I could get a horse to turn out exactly how I wanted him to be because he would have no lasting baggage for me to overcome.

Walt asked me if I wanted to go along with him and Amos to look at a horse. The owner had called them up and said he was having a few problems and was ready to send the horse away for dog meat. Walt told the fellow they'd be happy to have a look at the horse and maybe even take him off his hands.

When we got there I found myself looking at a very worried Warm-blood gelding. He was agitated and kept pushing into the fellow holding the lead rope. Walt suggested he let the horse go in one of the nearby square yards normally used for cattle. While we leaned over the top rail and watched the horse work himself into a lather of sweat in the yard, Walt and

Amos asked the owner all about the horse. He told us that he owned the horse for nearly a year and then rattled off a list of problems he had with the horse. The list contained everything from float loading to shying problems. The way the fellow was talking you could tell he had enough of this horse and felt he had been ripped off by the previous owner. He just wanted to be rid of the horse and was going to buy a new one. He said that this time he was not going to make the same mistake as before. He was going to buy a young unbroken horse and have it trained from scratch. He reckoned that by buying a horse like that he was sure not to buy a horse with problems and everything should go much smoother.

Walt and Amos decided to take the horse off the fellow and agreed to give him the same price as the meat fellows would pay. While Walt was paying the fellow, Amos and I got the horse loaded into the back of the truck. As we pulled out of the driveway, Walt said to the fellow that we will see him next time. I didn't know what he meant. What next time?

It was clear that this horse was definitely a project, but he had a kind nature and was a quick learner. Walt renamed him Popcorn because he kept having tiny explosions at little things. It took a couple of months, but between Amos and me we were able to build some confidence and trust into the horse. Gradually the horse learned not to explode and that yielding to a human's idea was not going to kill him. Once this got accomplished the softness started coming through his body and his mind. Eventually, Walt found a buyer for Popcorn that would suit him well and Walt and Amos made a larger than small profit.

A few more months passed before the same fellow who had owned Popcorn called Walt. This time he had a young filly that he had bought just after he sold the Warmblood. He had it broken in and had been riding it for about three months. Initially, things had gone pretty well but now the filly was becoming a bit more of a handful. Like the Warmblood, the filly was shying, but bigger. She also wouldn't stand still to be saddled or mounted and the farrier had been kicked by her. The owner felt the filly had a really bad nature and he had been ripped off by the breeder who sold her with the promise that she was a quiet and unspoiled horse.

Well, it was another trip to the fellow's property. Walt had a quick scan of the filly and did a deal that seemed to suit them both. Again, I helped Amos load the horse into the truck. On the way home I asked Walt and Amos why this fellow had so much trouble with his horses.

"Well matey, it's because he don't know that horses have their own way of doin things," was the response I got from Walt.

"Huh," I said?

"He just thinks horses should do what he tells them to do and when they don't he just tells them louder. It don't make them understand him any better, but it gets them pretty worried," Amos replied.

I wanted to ask another question. "So it didn't make any difference that this time he bought a young green horse? Because he said he was going to buy a horse that nobody else had messed up. But he had just as many problems with this horse as he did with Popcorn."

"No, it don't make no difference," Walt said. "He messed up the young un all by himself and he can take credit for a good chunk of the trouble the Warmblood was in, too."

This time it was Amos who opened my eyes to a new idea.

"See matey, lots of people blame the problems they have with a horse on the horse's history. Ya know, they say things like he don't float load too good because he had a floatin accident three years ago. Well that was three years ago! What the hell are ya doin blamin somethin on what happened three years ago?" Amos snorted and shook his head.

"And this notion that gettin a young unspoiled horse will lessen the risk of havin problems later is rubbish. If ya don't know how to fix a floatin problem, ya don't know how to teach it right in the first place. It takes just as much skill to put the right idea in a horse's head in the first place as it does to change a bad idea into a good idea. That's not to say it ain't easier to stop a problem before it happens. But it takes the same skill and awareness. And if ya ain't got that skill and awareness, buying a young unhandled horse isn't goin to save ya from trouble down the road."

So that dispelled another myth for me. Amos had burst my bubble. I thought I could become a really good horse starter and leave the really dangerous behaviour of the older horses alone. There was no point in just starting horses because to become a top notch horse breaker I would also have to be a top notch problem solver. Amos was telling me that one was the same as the other.

As always, Walt had the final say.

"Ya know matey, most of the time all me and Amos do when we work with a horse is try to convince them that the human ain't quite as stupid and dangerous as the horse really thinks he is and that ain't easy because often times it ain't true."

WHAT DOES IT MEAN TO BE IN CONTROL?

Walt and Amos were in their seventies when I was in my early and middle teens. Despite their strange eccentricities, I had never met anybody who understood or felt so much about horses. I reckon these old men were the closest humans could come to being part horse. They saw so much and felt so much about what was going on inside a horse that they hardly ever got into an argument with a horse. They knew exactly what even the most troubled horse needed at any instant and they were always right there for their friend.

I say friend because to Amos and Walt that is what every horse was - he was a friend. I think a large part of their secret with horses was that they never saw any horse as other than an equal. Today trainers talk about dominance and submission, alpha horses and herd behaviour. But for the old men there was never any talk about who was boss and who was in control. To them, working with a horse was a co-operative venture. They approached each horse with an open heart, with no bias, no prejudice and no pre-conceived judgments. I reckon this is what made them different from every other horse person I have known. Walt and Amos never saw themselves as better than any horse they were working. They never viewed themselves as being in charge or having control of the horse. Working with a horse was a partnership for these old men.

I remember one day overhearing Amos talking to a woman in her middle years. No doubt Amos thought she was no more than a young girl. The woman had sent her thoroughbred filly to the brothers for help. She described moments of terror on the occasions her filly had bolted out of control while cantering in both the arena and on the trail. The lady presumed the behaviour was a remnant of the filly's racing days. To make her point, she rode the horse in the arena, and sure enough, half a dozen strides into the canter the horse was running out of control and the woman had to point her into the fence to stop her. She had tried every bit in the saddlery shop and now had more hardware hanging in her tack room than a Mitre 10 warehouse. Although some bigger bits had helped for awhile, it wasn't long before the filly was ignoring the woman's efforts to stop with even these monster devices. She had taken her horse to a handful of trainers who had tried bits, martingales, running reins, all sorts of gear, but these achieved no more than a short term kind of success. It seemed that the old men were the filly's last chance. If they couldn't reform her behaviour she was going to the market.

I was very keen to watch how Amos was going to help this lady. I had never seen either of the brothers tackle a seriously bolting horse or even a horse with a hard mouth. This was going to be a lesson to remember. It did worry me a little to think that Amos was going to ride a potential bolter. Even though I guessed he was fairly fit for a man in his middle seventies, he was well passed his physical prime and I doubted he would have the strength to pull up a horse that was committed to running away.

For a few days Amos virtually ignored the filly. He would enter her yard only to feed and pet her. Sometimes he would hang around the outside of the yard and just watch for awhile, then walk away. I once asked him what he was watching for and he said, "Nothin. Just hidin 'way from Walt!" I knew better than to ask anymore. In the months and years to come I did learn what Amos was really watching for and it became an integral part of my practice when I started working horses on my own. But that's another tale for another time.

I was beginning to wonder if Amos was ever going to work the filly when one day about a week after she arrived, he went out to the yard with a halter and lead rope over his arm. I quit doing my favourite job of cleaning stables and went over to watch. Amos caught the horse and petted her for awhile, then led her over to the arena. He did some ground work with her for about 40 minutes. Nothing I hadn't seen the brothers do a zillion times before with all sorts of horses. I already knew about disengaging the hindquarters, about getting a horse's focus, about softening the horse all the way through from his nose to his hocks. I watched Amos work away at getting all these things done with the filly and witnessed the transformation from a tight "ready to flee" animal to a horse who was giving Amos all her attention, ready for his next move.

Once these changes happened, Amos reached for his saddle that was hanging on the fence.

Saddling posed a small problem for this horse, but Amos soon had the horse soft and composed with his usual quiet patience. He led the horse around for awhile and he proceeded to mount. I realized instantly that Amos had forgotten to fit a bridle. No doubt his ancient brain was getting forgetful.

"Amos, you forgot the bridle. I'll go and get it for you," I interrupted.

"Don't botha matey. She'll do fine as she is."

I couldn't believe that Amos was about to get on a horse with a serious bolting problem with only a halter for control. How was he ever going to get out of trouble when she started to take off on him? He was too old to bail out and too frail to pull the horse to a stop in only a halter. I figured there was some serious trouble just ahead and wondered if I should go and find Walt to talk some sense into his baby brother.

As soon as Amos straddled the filly's back, her head arched upwards, her back hollowed and she began to prance a little. I watched as Amos sat there as quiet as can be, and began to lift the lead rope and wait. After a minute or so the filly's head dropped and she walked on quietly as Amos let go of the rein. He then flipped the lead rope over the other side of her neck and did the same. In no more than 30 minutes, that horse was walking and trotting around that arena as soft and calm as could be with her head hanging level with her withers and her feet moving smartly across the sand. Amos could turn her, stop her and back her up, all with just a lead rope. It was quite a demonstration and a huge change from when the owner rode her.

But I knew the real test would come when Amos asked for the canter. The lady said her filly only bolted in the canter. I didn't have long to wait. I didn't know what Amos did, but the horse began to canter around the arena. That was pretty typical of these old men. They hardly ever did anything to get a horse to respond. It was like telepathy, but I learned later it was really about timing the requests. Anyway, the horse cantered as nicely as she had walked and trotted - just like she was off to do her shopping for the week. She was a little crooked in her circles and kept side-stepping at one corner, but this was the most impressive demonstration I had seen.

Over the next few days, Amos continued to ride the horse in the arena in only a halter. But by the fifth day he was riding her out on the trail - again with only a halter and saddle. Two weeks passed before he put a bridle with a plain snaffle bit in her mouth.

I continued to be bothered by why Amos didn't put a bridle on the horse from the first ride. I knew Amos would have a simple answer that would make me feel like an idot, but I couldn't help myself, I had to know what he knew.

"Amos, why didn't you ride that horse with a bit on the first day if you knew she could bolt?"

"Well matey, if she'd 'ave got to runnin, no bit was goin to save me. That poor thing had every bit they'd ever made in her mouth at some time and all that done was scare her about folks pullin on her mouth," came the reply.

"But how was there any way you could control her with just a web halter and a lead rope?" I asked.

Amos then said one of the most profound things that I can ever remember coming from this horsemen's horseman.

"Son, control is somethin ya don't impose on a horse. Control is somethin a horse gives ya. Horses are bigger, stronger, faster and prettier than any people I know. If I want me horse to respond with the lightness of a butterfly wing, nothin will give that to me 'cept a horses mind. Nothin bought in a shop will give me that kind of control."

At the time, I didn't realize the importance of Amos' words. It has taken years and thousands of mistakes to teach me the lesson that Amos told me in those few seconds all those years ago. I guess I wasn't ready to know it then and I had to wait until I had a better understanding of the inside of a horse and what horsemanship is all about.

Amos once said to me, "The difference between horsemanship and good horsemanship is the difference between having a horse work for you and having a horse work with you." This is the legacy that these two old men left me.

BETWEEN A ROCK
AND HARD PLACE!

A couple of years ago I was giving one of my regular monthly demonstrations. It was a cold Friday night and a very nice couple had brought their quarter horse gelding along. I had never seen the horse before, but I was told that the people had owned him for nearly two years and in that time they had always had trouble giving him worm paste. When the owners approached the horse with a syringe of wormer he would toss his head and run backwards. If he couldn't get away he would finally resort to rearing. It had been a major headache for the owners and they felt they had tried everything they could think of doing to fix the problem. When they purchased the horse their first attempt to worm paste him resulted in them grabbing the ear. But on the second try that didn't work and they then used a nose twitch. In subsequent weeks and months they discovered that each new method they tried only worked once and they had to keep thinking of new techniques. This resulted in the use of a lip string, pinching a skin fold in the neck, a pasting bit and tying up a leg. One after the other these methods were tried on him, but each time he would get more and more violent. The last approach caused such a violent reaction in the horse that the owners finally resorted to having a vet sedate the horse. But again this had its problems because they then learned that the horse had an equally violent reaction to being given a needle. The whole thing had caused the owners great despair and in their desperation a friend had talked them into allowing a local trainer to look at their horse as part of a demonstration. That's how come I came to see the horse.

When I first looked at the horse I saw a horse that deliberately tried to turn his attention away from the owners. He knew they were there, but he seemed to figure that if he didn't pay attention to them they would go away and all his troubles would be over. I knew exactly what was going on with this horse because I had seen it before - many times.

I was first made aware of this type of problem when I was a kid. I had just started a horse for a woman who wanted a nice trail horse. This was exactly the type of horse for her. His name was Slingshot. He was kind, smart and brave. He didn't have too much go. Nor was he too much of a slug. It took quite a bit to make him nervous or shy which was unusual for a horse so young and inexperienced. He was perfect for the owner who was a bit of a nervous rider.

Slingshot had been out on a few trail rides and was handling the going really well. There had been quite a bit of rain in the last day or so and the trail was a little slippery. Slingshot and I were traveling down the trail at an easy pace when I felt him suddenly tense up. He stopped with his weight on his hind end ready to start back peddling as fast as he could. We had come around a corner to find water running across the trail. It wasn't flowing fast, but he had never seen still water let alone moving water before. I kicked him on. But Slingshot darted left, then right. I kicked him again and he started running back. I got more and more insistent that he go forward and eventually he leaped over the water. I turned him back towards the water and he leapt again. There were several repetitions and although he eventually got his feet into the water he stayed a little tense.

Over the following days, I took Slingshot down that same trail and we had to negotiate the small stream each day. Every day he had to stop and back-peddle until I got so assertive that he had no choice but to go forward. I would take him back and forward until he felt better about the water, but this change never held. Every day he reacted just like he did the first time.

After about five days of dealing with Slingshot's problem with water and getting no lasting improvement I decided to talk to Walt. I found him unscrewing the cap off his beaten up old thermos, about to pour himself a cuppa. He had one foot on the bottom rail of the fence and was looking at his horse, Burner, cavorting around the paddock. I went up next to him and mimicked his pose. He didn't even look at me as he poured his tea, but asked what was up. I told Walt what had happened with Slingshot and the water across the trail and what I had been doing about it.

"Walt, how come he hasn't learned that it is just water and no big deal? Why does he put on a show about it every time? I mean he has gone through it maybe forty times now and he still thinks he has to fuss about it."

"Well matey, it seems pretty simple to me. You've done everythin to confirm Slingshot's worst fears," was Walt's response.

"How," I asked?

"When Slingshot first saw the water he didn't know what it was. It was slitherin and bubblin and gurglin across a path he knew had never had such a thing on before. He figured it was maybe goin to kill him, so he got worried and wanted to get as far away from it as he could. Next thing he knows you are whackin him with ya leg and rein to make him get near that thing. He wasn't sure if the water was goin to kill him or you was goin to kill him. Either way he knew he was goin to die - he just had to decide whether it was to be by water or by whackin. He was just doin the best he could, given that you put him between a rock and hard place."

"Every time he was faced with that water problem, you kept gettin him in trouble with tryin to make him go forward. Ya never got him to feel that the water was no bother to him 'cause every time he saw it you was always kickin and yankin on him. From the start he figured the water was trouble and you just proved it to him every single time that he was right. That's why he don't get no better about the water. Ya gotta find a way that Slingshot can negotiate the water and find out for himself that he was carryin on about nothing. Let him feel stupid for putting on such a fuss about a silly bit of water. It's that same ol' problem me and Amos have been tellin ya about since I can't remember how long. Don't try to make it happen. Set it up so it can happen. If you ask a horse to deal with his fears and then beat him up for being afraid – you'll just confirm in his own mind that he was right to be afraid."

I had a pretty sleepless night thinking about what Walt had said. It took no more than another three rides before Slingshot had learned that the running water was ok. But it took me a few more years to learn what Walt had been trying to teach me about putting a horse between a rock and a hard place and then expecting him to make a change for the better. That's what I was recalling while I was watching the quarter horse gelding at the demonstration.

I asked the owners to show me and the audience what happened when they tried to worm paste the horse. The poor fellow ran the whole gamut of behaviour they had described - including the rearing. I finally asked them if they would mind if I had a try. First, I did a little bit of ground handling to ensure I had the horse's attention. When he was ready, I put my thumb in his mouth and removed it even before he knew what had happened. I repeated it, but the horse was ready and began to toss his head. I just kept my thumb in his mouth until there was a split second when he stopped tossing. This was the moment he was trying to decide "what was the next strategy he needed to try". At that moment I removed my thumb. Again I repeated the whole procedure and removed my thumb at exactly the right moment. After a few minutes he didn't toss his head or run backwards when I placed my thumb in his mouth and left it there. He tried to play with my thumb using his tongue, but he was very polite about it. It was at this point that I introduced an empty syringe into his mouth while my thumb was still in place. It didn't bother him at all. I repeated this several times without a problem. Finally, I took a real syringe filled with worm paste and repeated what I had already done. When he was standing quietly I simply squirted the paste into the back of the throat and removed the syringe. I left the horse alone for a few minutes while he digested what had just happened. Shortly after that I asked the owners to go up and pretend to squirt worm paste into the horse's mouth just like they had seen me do. I had to adjust the way they used their hand a little bit, but the horse stood quietly and accepted the syringe once again into the back of his mouth. This went really well, but it left me with a problem. How to fill in the remaining one and half hours of a two hour demonstration!

The horse had learned that worm pasting was a bad deal because life always took a turn for the worse when people showed up with that syringe. At the start he knew that worm-pasting was something he should be bothered about. It was a strange sensation to have somebody stick a foreign object into his mouth, so he tossed his head and probably even stepped backwards. But then people started to get heavy-handed with him and grab an ear or put a twitch on him and now he was convinced he was really in trouble and maybe even going to die. Then purely by accident he noticed that if he got really violent about what was happening the people with the syringe would go away and leave him alone. He learned that every time they got more determined, all he had to do was get more determined and violent and life got better. That's how his behaviour became so strongly instilled. He was taught to be difficult to worm paste by people. It was just the same problem where I had I started to teach Slingshot to have a problem with water.

Horses don't bite, kick, rear, toss their heads, run you down, pin their ears, etc., because it is fun or because they are out to get you. They have their reasons, and they are always genuine reasons. We may not understand their reasons and that is often when we say they are just being pigs or they are doing it deliberately. But it is a mistake to assume those things because it leads to the sorts of mistakes that those people made with the quarter horse and that I made with Slingshot. Don't make it any harder than necessary on a horse. Always try to make the option you want them to choose the easiest option. You should not try to make the wrong thing so difficult that it is almost impossible. There is a huge difference between making the wrong response so hard that they can't choose it and making the right response so easy that they want to choose it. That's the difference between the way I handled Slingshots problem with water and the way Walt wanted me to handle it.

MAKE YOUR IDEA
YOUR HORSE'S IDEA

Stella was a Paint mare Walt had picked up at an auction sale. She was about seven years old and Walt thought she had probably had at least one foal. He had bought her really cheap and had plans to work her to sell again. This is how the old brothers often supplemented their meagre incomes and they were good at it.

I use to feed Stella and clean her yard on weekends and got to like the mare. She was nervous of new things, but smart enough to quickly evaluate their danger to her or not. She had been at the riding school for about three weeks before Walt finally got around to deciding he had better put some time into her before she was no longer a cheap horse. He asked me if I would like to help with training Stella and I could not have been keener.

Walt told me to get Stella and take her into the round yard and we would start with seeing what was going on inside her. I haltered Stella and led her out of her yard. She was a bit pushy to lead and was trying to take me for a walk rather than the other way around. I finally got her into the round yard and waited for Walt to show up. Stella kept walking around me and was not in the least interested in my presence. Eventually Walt showed up and saw me holding a very fidgety horse.

"Well matey, what are ya goin to do with her now," he asked?

"What do you want me to do, Walt?"

"Ya might start with gettin her feelin betta so she can pay attention to ya," he said. "Why don't ya take off that head collar and let her go for a bit?"

I removed the halter and Stella trotted to the opposite side of the yard closer to where she could see other horses. I looked at Walt as if to ask "now what".

"Now matey, take about three feet from the end of ya lead rope and whack the ground as hard as ya can. But don't try to drive her anywhere, just whack the ground. Maybe whack it behind ya so she don't think ya tryin to hit her."

I did as Walt told me, but nothing happened. Stella was too focussed on the other horses to notice.

"No matey, I mean whack it hard on the ground. Cause an earthquake if ya can."

I tried again. This time I gave it everything I had. Stella jumped and took off running around the track.

"Now stand there matey. Don't do anything – just let her work this out," Walt ordered.

I stood there passively and watched Stella run several lapse around the pen. After about the fifth lap she suddenly stopped where she could see the other horses and then ran the other way. Another lap and she stopped again close to where the horses were. This time she stood looking out of the yard at the horses.

"Time to whack again, matey – but not so hard," Walt told me.

I whacked the ground behind me just enough to cause a tremor rather than a fully blown quake. Stella took off again in the pen. But this time after about the first lap she slowed down and finally stopped and looked at me.

"Now matey, don't do anythin just yet – just wait."

A minute or so went by. Stella looked back towards her horsey friends.

"Let her look for a bit, but if ya think she ain't goin to look back at ya, whack the ground again. But only half as much as last time," Walt suggested.

Stella did not check back with me after about half a minute. This time I gently whacked the side of my leg with the lead rope. Stella walked off about half a lap of the yard, stopped and looked at me. She only looked at me for a couple of seconds, but then sniffed the ground for a few seconds, then looked at me again. Then the little paint mare turned and walked the other way and stopped nearest to her friends. I just lifted the lead rope against my side and Stella walked around the yard until she was behind me. Then she stopped and squared up to me, looking at me with both eyes. One of the horses called and Stella looked that way for a second or two, then looked at me again and walked a step towards me.

"Ya doin great, matey. Now ya could go and pat her if ya wanted, but let's wait and see what she does next," I heard Walt suggest.

I must have stood there three minutes thinking nothing was going to change before I saw Stella shift her weight onto her rear end and take another two steps towards me. I waited some more to see how far I could take this. Eventually after another few minutes Stella tentatively walked towards me and stopped within patting distance. I raised my hand to pat her.

"Don't touch her, matey. Just stand there for a bit. I'll let ya know when to pat her."

I waited and I waited until eventually Walt gave me the ok to touch her.

The session went on for a little while longer and we built on the liberty work to get it a little stronger and make a change in how Stella felt. After Stella was back in her own yard I set about picking Walt's brains about what we just did.

"Ya ask hard questions, matey. So much went on in that short time that ya could fill a book," Walt said.

"When Stella came into the yard she was all prancy and fussy. Then ya let her go and she went to the other side of the yard closer to them other horses. Why did she do that?"

"I guess she was nervous, Walt," I said.

"She did it matey, 'cause bein with you in that yard felt bad to her and bein nearer them other horses was a better choice to her. We needed to change that. We could 'ave put her back on the halter and made her do what we wanted, but they ain't goin to change how she feels inside so it was always goin to be a battle between her needs and our wants. The best result would be to change how she felt about our wants. Let her make the choice that bein with ya is better deal than with them other horses. Let it be her choice, but let it be the choice we want too.

When that mare got her attention fixed on them horses and not you, ya whacked the ground and gave her somethin else to think about. She ran, but ya didn't make her run 'cause ya did nothin more than if a tractor went by. Ya didn't chase her around to run. She ran until runnin no longer felt good to her. Then she stopped runnin and went back to paying attention to them horses. Ya whacked again and she thought that was not too good and left them horses again. This kept up until she worked out that when she was lookin at them horses, there was energy in the pen and when she slowed and checked in with ya it was all pretty quiet. Soon enough she thought she might try to stick near ya and see if it was a better choice. But ya never made anythin happen. Ya never ran her around and around until she was desperate to try anythin else – even being with ya. She made all the choices. Ya just weighted them choices a little in favour of what ya wanted. Ya never once directed her to run or come to you or look at the horses. All ya did was give her a reason to keep searchin for somethin that was better than she was already tryin.

It's the difference between makin a horse choose between somethin that is hard and somethin that is harder or choosin between somethin is easy and something that is just a little less easy. If you make what ya want the easy choice – so easy that he would even choose it with no help from you – then he will feel good about workin with ya. But if ya just make his choices between hard and harder nothin will feel ok to him – everythin he does is troublin in one way or another – and he gives you everythin you ask for with reluctance and resistance."

"But why did you tell me to wait before patting her, Walt? Shouldn't I have gone in and rewarded her with a pat as soon as possible," I asked?

"Well matey, that mare made the choice to take a few steps towards you. She weren't sure, but she figured that nothin else was workin too good so she would try checkin in with ya and see if that worked for her. When a horse is teeterin on the edge of what she should or should not do, don't rush in and do somethin that might get her thinkin she made the wrong decision. The mare weren't totally sure that bein with ya was a good idea. She needed time to get sure. Let her get secure with her idea. Don't invade her space. Wait until she is feelin better. If she had wanted ya in her face she would have come right up to ya instead of standin three feet away. But then somethin changed and she got sure. She looked at you with both eyes, her breathing slowed, her ears stopped twitching back and forth to them other horses and her weight got planted on her front. That's when I knew she was ready to accept ya in closer to pat her with a good feelin."

I got to spend more time with Walt and Stella and I learned a lot about allowing a horse to make the choices I would like them to choose rather than making them choose what I want. It's hard to keep clear and sometimes the constraints of training for the public limits how much time you can allow a horse to work things out without some stronger prompting. But Walt understood better than anybody I have known how a horse's feelings are connected to everything they do.

FIXING THE GAP

The horse's name was Merrick. Walt and Amos bought him from a fellow that was selling up his property and stock to move to warmer climates in Queensland. He was no beauty and he looked much older than you would expect for a nine year old thoroughbred/quarter horse gelding. He arrived about 70 kg too light and looking depressed. I wondered if the old brothers had got a good deal or not.

Merrick had been given a week or so to settle in before Amos started to spend some time with him on ground manners and leading. He was a horse that liked to drag on the end of the lead rope. He dragged to come forward and he dragged to find a stop. It took Amos a couple of days to get Merrick to stop leaning on the lead rope and to follow his feel in coming forward, backward and in a turn. Every chance I got between cleaning stables and saddles I watched Amos working with Merrick. It was always an education to see them at work. I never got tired of studying Amos with a horse no matter how many times I had seen him teach horses to lead.

When the ground work showed significant improvement, Amos got Merrick dressed in an old beat up stock saddle and a side-pull (a kind of bitless bridle) to avoid causing Merrick pain from a bit. The first ride was not pretty to watch. Merrick really didn't have much idea how to stop from the reins, not because he didn't have a bit in his mouth, but because he was use to leaning on the reins just like he leaned on the lead rope.

Merrick's initial response to the use of Amos' leg was to tuck his behind in and scoot forward. One could only guess that perhaps Merrick had been spurred quite a lot in order to teach him to go forward. The result was an explosive forward from worry and tension rather than a soft response to the leg. The turns were also a problem. Merrick struggled to bend through his turns and ran out through the shoulder. All in all, this was not a horse that was going very well under saddle.

A couple of weeks passed before Amos took Merrick on a trail ride. He asked that I saddle up Walt's horse, Burner, and go with him. As we passed through the front gate Merrick was leading the way. He seemed settled and happy to be going somewhere. A couple of hundred metres down the rode Amos told me to go past him and stop at the tree ahead. I asked Burner to trot past and saw Merrick trying to go with me. Amos bent him to the left to slow his feet as I got further away. When I arrived at the tree I turned my horse to see Amos struggling hard to settle his horse. Merrick was prancing with his head up and back hollow. Amos kept asking him to yield his forehand to the left and the right. When I realized what a big struggle Amos was having I made my way back to him. When I got within about 10 metres of them Merrick started to make a change and settle. We walked with both horses side by side for awhile. Then Amos told me to leave again and go about 50 metres away. Again Merrick tensed up and tried to come with me. Amos kept control of the situation with his amazing timing and feel. He then asked that I come back. As I got closer, Merrick relaxed even more. Amos and I repeated this exercise over and over again. Merrick continued to improve his behaviour whenever Burner and I went ahead. Eventually I was able to go several hundred metres ahead and come back while Amos had Merrick walking. Over the coming days I rode out a lot with Amos, and soon Merrick could calmly walk, trot and canter in front or behind. It didn't matter if Amos left me behind or I left him behind. Merrick showed very little of the monster-like behaviour of that first ride.

It was a couple of months after Walt and Amos had bought Merrick that a woman named Elaine arrived to look at the horse. She was in the market for a trail horse. She didn't want anything too dull, but she wanted a horse that was safe. Amos caught Merrick and got him saddled. He rode the horse in the arena and showed how soft and responsive Merrick was to ride. Amos then suggested Elaine ride him. Merrick did all the right things for her although she seemed to ride with a bit more contact than normal and she had the habit of gripping her legs to his sides. Merrick's response was to hollow out just a fraction more than normal and to get busy with his mouth, but nothing that would normally concern a rider. Amos made some suggestions on riding him with a softer contact and to relax her legs and Merrick really appreciated the difference. Amos then took Elaine out on a trail ride. It must have gone well because she seemed very happy when they returned. There was some haggling about price, but an agreement was soon made that appeared to satisfy them both. Then Elaine asked if she could get a vet check and assuming the horse passed she would like to pick up Merrick the next weekend.

Everything went well with the vet inspection and Merrick was trucked to his new home the following week. About a month passed when the phone rang at the riding school. It was Elaine who was calling to tell Amos that she was not happy with Merrick at all and she was bringing him back the next day and expected a full refund of her money. The truck pulled up as scheduled and I remember how mad Elaine was. Amos quietly waited until she stopped her tirade. She said the horse was sold without telling her how dangerous he could be to ride. The gist of it was that she had taken Merrick on a few trail rides and he had gotten more and more difficult to control. The last straw was a few days earlier when she rode with a friend. Her friend's horse went ahead of Merrick and Merrick tried to go with him. Elaine tried to stop Merrick from rushing forward and he started to prance on the spot. She kicked him to go forward and the horse bucked her off. Amos said that he would ride the horse for her now and she could ride his old horse. As they left for the trail I could see that Merrick was not the quiet soft horse he had been a month ago. Amos later told me that he was a handful for about three or four minutes, but then he settled really well. Merrick showed no sign of the trouble Elaine talked about after Amos had ridden him for a bit. They then changed horses on the way home. Amos said that it took Merrick less than ten minutes to start prancing again with Elaine riding him. They changed horses again and Amos rode him the rest of the way home.

After Amos had given her a refund and Elaine had gone home I asked him what went wrong with Merrick. I said that Merrick was such a nice horse and he was riding so well that I was surprised that Elaine had problems with him.

'Well matey, people think that when you teach a horse somethin that they know it forever. Horses act in response to what the human does. If ya teach a horse to stop with a soft ask on them reins, he only stops nicely if ya ask him to stop usin them reins in the same way that he was taught. If ya use them in a different way he won't know what they mean."

"So Amos are you saying that Elaine was not riding Merrick like you ride Merrick and therefore he was behaving differently?"

"Yeah, that's right matey. Ya see ya never actually fix a problem. Ya don't work on a problem with a horse and then it goes away and expect it will never raise its ugly head agin. It ain't like that. The problem is still always there. But ya learn to manage the problem by ridin or handlin ya horse in a different way. That lady rode Merrick in a way that brought all his ol' habits to the surface agin. Anybody that rides him like that will have the same problem. I can't fix the horse that has a problem with poor ridin to behave great when he's ridden poorly. Instead ya manage the problem by learnin to ride properly for that horse."

"Is that true with any problem a horse can have, Amos?"

"You bet, matey. Don't matter if it's catchin him or loadin him in a float or jumpin him around a course. If ya got a horse with a hard mouth ya don't fix it by hangin onto his mouth with ya reins. Ya ride with earlier releases of the reins and a softer feel. When he gets a soft mouth he won't stay soft if ya tighten up those reins agin. Instead ya manage the problem by always ridin him with a soft feel and early releases. That way ya will never have to haul on his mouth to get him to stop agin."

Amos was right. You never do fix a problem, you just manage it. A horse (and a rider) is always a work in progress. They are never finished and they never stop learning the good and bad stuff.

CONFIDENCE AND HORSES

Confidence and overcoming nervousness around horses seems to be a very common issue in the horse world. In my capacity as a trainer who starts horses for people and helps them with horses that present with difficult behaviourial problems, I meet a lot of folk who have had a scare from their horse and who have a lot of trouble regaining their confidence. It is something that very many people struggle with and torments them continuously.

Most people have a theory for their loss of confidence. The most common one that I hear is "as a kid nothing would bother me. I'd ride my pony without a bridle or a saddle and jump off a thousand foot cliff and land upside down into a raging river. Then canter down the rapids until we came to the sea and swim to Tassie for lunch, fighting off white pointers all the way and have so much fun doing it. But since I got married and had kids I can't afford to get hurt and now I'm afraid to lead my horse from the paddock."

While I don't doubt that kids are generally more "gung ho" than adults, I'm not sure I believe that having kids is what turns our legs into jelly at the thought of getting on our horses. I say this because I see just as many women with confidence issues that have never had families or whose families have grown up and no longer need mum for their survival as I do those with young families. I also see a lot of kids who are afraid of their horses too. Some of this fear is perfectly justified because I too wouldn't want to get on some of those horses. But a lot of the fear is not based on anything the horse is presenting, but more based on peoples fear of the "what if" scenario. The fear of "what if" something goes wrong is a very powerful paralysing agent – stronger than curare for some people. I remember talking to Amos about fear and "what if" and thought he had some valuable things to say.

I had been riding for a few years and had come off plenty of times, but I had never been hurt. Then one day I was riding a horse over some jumps. I was riding bareback and the jumps were getting in the three and a half foot range. After about four jumps, I was approaching a triple spread fence. One stride from the fence Orpheus slammed on the brakes and stopped. Unfortunately, I didn't stop and was catapulted head first into the fence. The result was three days in hospital with a minor concussion. I was about fourteen and it was the first time I discovered I could be hurt. On doctors orders I was banned from riding for two weeks, but parental orders made that a lifetime ban. After a lot of continuous badgering and nagging, on my part, my folks finally gave in after a month. So finally, I was able to return to the riding school after my accident.

I felt fine and happy to be back – even cleaning stables was fun again. But when it came to time to ride a horse again I realized I was a bit nervous. What if I fell off again? Would I have permanent brain damage? Would it hurt again? I took the first few rides easy and rode one of the quiet horses. But it didn't seem to help me get over my initial fear. Each time I went to saddle a horse my heart would beat faster. I kept having images of being pile driven into the ground. This was not fun.

A couple of weeks after returning to the riding school I was talking to Amos about general stuff. When there was a lull in the conversation I asked him THE QUESTION!

"Amos, have you ever been scared of a horse?

"Matey, if a fella ain't ever been scared, then he ain't ever ridden enough horses."

"Well, what about Walt? Has he ever been scared?"

"Walt!! He's the biggest chicken I know. He gets scared ridin on one of them merry-go-rounds at the show. If he goes to the store, he can't even make himself go and pet one of them horses that ya put a coin into for kids to ride. Yep, poor ol Walt is a bundle of nerves around horses."

Hmmm. Was I sensing some sibling rivalry here?

"Well, Amos why do people get scared of horses?"

"Matey, 'cause if ya do somethin stupid they can hurt ya. People are always doin stupid things around horses, so they are smart to be scared of them."

I guess that made sense to me. If I stopped doing stupid things like jumping a horse I didn't really know without a saddle and around a course I hadn't practiced I wouldn't be trying to re-arrange jump rails with my head.

"But Amos, once you've had your confidence knocked how to do you get it back?" I asked.

"Well matey, I reckon there are two things ya need to stay safe. Once ya have these two things mastered, you'll have the confidence to know that ya can handle what ever comes ya way. It seems to me that people get scared because they can't predict what is goin to happen and they can't turn a horse off when they need to. But if a person learns to know what is goin to happen before it happens and then learns how to change the outcome from a bad one to a safe one, then they will have the confidence to know that they can control the situation and keep themselves and their horse safe. It is the lack of sureness about how to control a situation that gets people scared. Change that and people learn they ain't got nothin to fear.

A lot of people get scared matey and they try things like breathin exercises and picturin relaxin things with their minds. But those things are temporary fixes that go out the window the moment a horse does somethin like shies because they have not learned that they can interrupt the shy before it happens. When they learn that they will have the confidence in knowin that they can control the shy and nothin terrible is goin to happen to them."

"So Amos, how do I – I mean how does a person learn those things?"

"It's simple, but it ain't easy matey. Just get better. Firstly, learn to feel of ya horse. Learn to know what's he thinkin. Don't just ride, oblivious to even the smallest change in him. Get with ya horse and get him with ya. Ya'll learn to know when his thoughts are leavin ya and when somethin is botherin him. A lot of people think they got buck off for no reason and it just came outa nowhere. They're wrong. It never comes from nowhere. And most times the horse has been tellin them for ages it was comin if they didn't do somethin about it. But they never listened and it just seemed like he bucked from nowhere. Even horses that buck when ya put ya foot in the stirrup were telling ya he was goin to do somethin probably from the time ya caught him. So learn to know these things and then learn to change it. So if a horse is thinkin about buckin, learn how to interrupt that thought and change it for him to a thought that works for both of ya.

Secondly, if ya get it wrong and ya make a mistake and ya push ya horse into the wrong side of trouble, learn how to shut it down so ya can start again. Most people are not very good at shuttin down the energy. They might stop the horse's feet, but his energy is still bubbling away and the instant he moves again he will explode. That's not the way. Learn to turn off the power switch in a horse so that ya can start over and ya'll keep safe."

I think Amos was right and is still right. The only way that I know to get back the confidence that has been lost is to learn to feel what is going to happen and then learn what to do about it. In that way, you can have the confidence that whatever is up ahead, it is in your power to control the outcome. The "what if" that paralyses many of us, stops having the power to paralyse because we have the confidence in the tools we have acquired to influence the outcome rather than be a victim of whatever the horse decides to do. But it is not surprising that many people have trouble regaining their confidence after a scare. I have never seen these skills taught by riding instructors or at club rally days. Very few books or videos deal with this topic. We try to teach the concepts and skills at our clinics, but in the end it behoves each horse person to understand the inside of their horse and learn what to do to stay on the correct side of trouble. As Amos said, "it simple, but it ain't easy."

RESPECT AND DISRESPECT IN HORSES

At one point in my time at the riding school Amos let me ride and compete on his horse called Bucky. Amos had broken in Bucky and had allowed me to ride him in a dressage clinic that I had won a scholarship to attend. I was desperately in need of a horse for the occasion and Amos was kind enough to lend me Bucky. Despite the fact that he had only been started a few weeks earlier, he did me, Amos and himself proud. Amos was so proud that he allowed me to keep riding Bucky and even enter a few competitions at local shows.

It was at local show that I had one of my early insights into the issue of respect and disrespect in horses. Walt and Amos were there. They had loaded Bucky and me into their old Ford truck. It was a temperamental beast and prone to giving up from exhaustion on some of the bigger hills. I never worked out which was older; the truck or the old brothers! But Amos had a way of coaxing the truck into keep trying its best – just like he did with his horses. We always got where we were going, but I sometimes wondered if we would get back from where we had been.

Once we arrived at the show, Amos went for a stroll to check out the sights like he always did while Walt helped me unload Bucky and get him ready. Amos returned with a show program and I hurried to get my entries done and paid for. When I got back from the stewards tent, a really large truck and trailer had parked next to us. They had about five horses on board and were unloading each of them to be tied up on the side nearest to our truck. On the side of their trailer in huge print was a fellow's name with a pronouncement that he was a trainer of show and performance horses. This got my interest and I watched as they unloaded each horse. There were a couple of showjumpers, a couple of show hacks and a filly that was obviously too young to be broken in – probably a yearling for the halter classes.

We had arrived in plenty of time for Bucky's events, so I asked Walt if he wanted to go and walk around. We wandered aimlessly towards the rings where the led classes were being held. There were certainly some nice looking horses and Walt and I discussed which ones we would like to smuggle into the back of the old Ford. One of the entrants was having a bit of trouble with their horse. He was a 2 year old colt. He was dancing around his owner and seemed to be unaware of her. She got pushed aside several times and even had her hat knocked off as the colt swung his head from side to side. She had a bridle on him and yanked it several times to get his attention and some semblance of control of his feet, but it didn't make too much difference. The colt's antics upset several of the other entrants and there were lots of mutterings from those around about an out of control colt. Several people were more than a little peeved at the owner's inability to control her horse. Nevertheless, the judging proceeded and of course the colt that was behaving so badly was summarily dismissed by the judge. When the judging finished and the horses were leaving the ring I saw the fellow who had parked the truck beside the old Ford walked towards the lady with the colt. He spoke to her for a moment and then gave her a card and pointed towards his truck.

It was getting time to get Bucky ready for our first event, so Walt and I went back to the Ford and got him brushed and saddled. After our event a lunch break was announced over the PA system. Walt broke out the beaten old thermos and Amos opened up a plastic box containing a selection of ham and tomato or egg and lettuce sandwiches. I really wanted a pie and coke from the kiosk tent, but I didn't feel right about that since the old men had gone to the trouble of providing lunch.

As we sat eating lunch and talking about the ride I had on Bucky or appraising the horses that paraded by during the break, the lady who owned the boisterous colt wandered up to speak to our trainer neighbour. All three of us sat quietly so we could hear what they were saying – but we pretended we weren't.

The lady was telling the fellow a bit of history about the colt and that she had always found him to be a handful when he would get distracted. She said he was lovely at home and was kind and gentle with no dirt. But if something got his attention or he got excited for some reason there was nothing she could do. He had broken her toe once when he spooked at something and jumped on her foot. The fellow listened politely and finally said that the problem is that her horse does not have much respect for her. He doesn't listen to her when he gets distracted because he does not view her as a person of importance. In her horse's eyes she was not at the top of the totem pole.

"Your horse sees you as below him in the pecking order and when he comes towards you or crowds you he thinks it is your job to get out of his way – just like if you were another horse that was below him in the pecking order. You would never see him crowd or step on a horse that was more dominant than your colt. That's because he respects them as being the boss and in charge. You need to learn to become the boss and turn his disrespect into respect."

At that point in my horsemanship I had never really thought about a person's relationship with a horse in terms of respect and disrespect. I had never heard the old men use those terms and since they were almost my only influence when it came to understanding horses I was wondering if I had missed out on a whole new world of concepts when it came to understanding horses. What the trainer fellow had told the lady made some sense when you think about how horses interact with other horses. There are clear boundaries between horses and a horse rarely over steps the mark with a more dominant horse.

The conversation between our neighbour and the lady continued, but I had to get Bucky ready for the next event so I missed out on what else was said. But I hadn't forgotten what the fellow had said and decided to bring the subject up with the old brothers on the trip home. But as usual the brothers were way ahead of me.

"So matey, ya had a pretty good day today. It would've been better if ya'd been a little more helpful in gettin Bucky to ride a line instead of goin around with no place in mind to go. Still ya done alright."

"I was pretty happy with Bucky, Walt," I said. "He does get a little lost and I know I have to get better timing for when his thought has gone. Still, the judges seemed to like him, especially the lady with the floral scarf."

"Well matey, as long as ya learned somethin," said Amos.

"What did ya think of that young colt, matey," asked Walt?

"I was wondering about what that fellow said about him not respecting the lady. Do you reckon that's right," I asked?

Walt answered with a question of his own. "What do ya think respect is, matey?"

"I don't know, Walt. I never thought about it."

"Well matey, if ya mean respect is treatin a person with politeness and courtesy, then I reckon that young'n had not much respect. But if ya think respect is treatin a person the way they deserve to be treated, then maybe that little colt had buckets of respect for the lady."

"Ya see matey, respect or no respect don't even enter a horse's mind. He has no idea of the concept. A horse reacts to any given situation based on how he feels about the situation – not about the person. He don't spend time figurin out if this person or that person deserves his respect or disrespect. He does was he does because of how a situation makes him feel. If he feels scared and overwhelmed because he feels there is more pressure than he can handle, then he is going to behave in some way to try save his life. That might mean crowdin the human or ignorin the fact they are even there. But it ain't about disrespectin the human, it's about doing what he feels he needs to do to save his life."

"So why do you say that the lady got what she deserved," I asked?

"Well matey, she did nothin to help the colt feel better. She hadn't done enough preparation before comin to the show to teach him to trust her that she wouldn't put him in a situation that might risk his survival. And when he did do his lolly, she just kept yankin his mouth which caused more pain and more fear and confirmed to the colt he really was in peril being there with her. So he did what he needed to do with no thought about respectin or disrespectin her – it doesn't even come into it. She put him in peril so he put her in peril – fairs, fair – simple as that. He gave her the respect she deserved."

"But Walt, what about what the fellow said about a horse respecting a more dominant horse, never crowding him or pushing on him etc." I asked?

"I still don't reckon respect comes into it, matey. No doubt there is a peckin order in every herd, but horses get there position in the herd by threatenin the weaker horses and submittin to the tougher horses. There ain't no more respect then there is between you and the school bully. Ya might give way to him and avoid gettin in his way, but ya don't like it and ya don't have nice things to say about him. It's more about survival than respect.

I think talkin about respect and disrespect when it comes to how a horse behaves is givin horses a value system that has no meanin to anybody but the human. I don't believe that Bucky went well today because last night he said to himself "that Ross is a good fellow, I'll try hard for him tomorrow." He went well 'cause you rode him the way ya did. If ya had rode him badly, he would have done badly. He just behaved in response to the way you rode. That little colt don't need a lesson in respect because he don't know what respect is. He just needs help to feel better and then he will behave better.

TO TRY OR NOT TO TRY

Walt and Amos had given me a horse to work. He was a bit of every breed and only stood about 14.2. They had bought him at an auction where the owner of an agistment paddock was selling any stock that belonged to people who hadn't paid their account for the last year. The old brothers figured he would make a nice type for just about anything. He was nothing special to look at, but he was sturdy and had a quiet disposition. The quality of handling had been pretty poor, because this little fellow was pushy and rude. But the brothers knew he would turn out all right with the proper education. My job was to re-mouth him. I was not to be paid for this task, but at the same time it meant there was no hurry. I guess Walt and Amos thought of it as part of their contribution to my education and if they happen to get some benefit out of it, then that was a happy coincidence.

I still remember the horse's name: Baz. He certainly had a hard mouth. Not only did he not stop when I picked up the reins, but he leaned even harder and got even faster. Because of such a strong brace I decided to ride him in the round yard for a bit until I got some sort of change. It just didn't feel like riding anywhere else was safe enough. At least in the round yard, if he took off I could ride as fast as he could run - as Amos was so fond of saying.

The first day I rode Baz he wore a plain snaffle bit. We began at the walk and tried getting some walk/halt transitions. Even here, I had to pull pretty hard to get him to stop his feet. After nearly an hour Amos made his way over to the yard to see how I was going. I mentioned that Baz was a hard case and I had only been making a small difference. Amos told me to keep going and he'd have a look.

"At least ya don't need no gym to join with the exercise ol' Baz is givin ya," was his first
comment.

"Let's make a couple of changes here," he said. "I want ya to stop pullin on his mouth. Next time ya want him to stop, pick up ya left rein a bit and wait until I tell ya to let go."

I walked Baz forward and after a few steps I picked up the left rein and he spun around.

"Too hard, matey. Just pick it up a little bit - enough so's he knows it's been picked up."

I repeated the procedure, but this time I slowly picked up the rein just enough to have taken the slack out of it. Immediately, I heard Amos shout, "release". It scared me. I wasn't expecting it because the horse hadn't stopped yet. But I released anyway. Amos told me to repeat it again and again and again. This went on for several minutes. I didn't know how much longer this futile exercise was going to continue. It seemed to me that I needed to get stronger if I was going to get Baz to make a change in his feet. I was about to say something to Amos in reference to the fact that nothing was happening when I suddenly realized that Baz had slowed to almost a stop when I picked up the rein again. I continued the exercise and within another three tries, Baz stopped as soon as he felt me pick up the rein. He didn't even wait until the rein tightened. I just had to shorten it a bit and he slowed his feet to a stop. He did this again.

I was more than a little surprised because I didn't understand why. How did Baz catch on so quickly, when he didn't learn anything when I got strong with the reins? There was something I was missing and I needed to ask Amos what it was.

"Well matey, ya missin the try. When ya was gettin strong with the reins, Baz was trying hard to listen, but ya was too busy waiting for the stop to know anythin about it. So he just kept on goin until it was too uncomfortable, then he'd stop his feet. When he was listenin ya weren't and when he wasn't listenin ya still weren't. He don't know what a soft rein means, so he only stopped to a hard rein."

"If ya offered him a soft rein and let it go as soon as he tries to listen, then ya gettin some
communication goin. I told ya pick up one rein and the first time I told ya to release was when he flicked his left ear back at ya. It told me he was listenin. He was tryin. Pretty soon when ya picked up that left rein he bent a little to the left and slowed his feet a little, so I got ya to let go. Pretty soon ya pick up that rein and he stop them feet. Every time Baz'd give ya a try ya need to let go. Let him know he's getting the right idea. No point in gettin strong when he's already tryin. He was tryin, but he just didn't understand. It'd be like ya teacher at school yellin and shoutin at ya when ya strugglin with a maths problem. As long as ya tryin, yellin and shoutin don't help. In fact, it might make ya learn to hate maths. Maybe that's how Baz feels about them reins."

Amos already anticipated my next question.

"Ya wanna know how ya know a horse is tryin? That ain't always easy, but as long as a horse has got his attention on ya and hasn't shut ya out of his mind, ya can be pretty sure he's tryin to figure a way out of his prob-lem. He may not be tryin the thing ya want him to try, but don't punish him for that."

"So if a horse has shut you out, is it ok to increase the pressure," I asked?

"Reckon it'd work for most horses," he replied.

"Then how do you know how much pressure is enough?"

"Well, ya wanna ask with just enough for it to mean somethin to the horse. Ya horse needs to regista that you've asked somethin of him. But it needs to be as little as it can be. That's how ya develop softness in a horse. The problem with Baz is that people ask too hard and they put a resistance in him. He learned that it didn't matter if he was soft or not 'cause people still used too much force, so he learned to shut down when people asked anythin of him. It's bin he's way of dealin with people who get too strong. Now he has to learn what it means when somebody asks him to do some-thin with hardly any force. It'll take a bit of doin, but he'll make it."

It took a few weeks of working with Baz before I began breaking down some of those barriers he had built. He gradually got softer and softer and eventually could go from a canter to a halt from just the seat. This was my first real experience at what Walt and Amos meant by "supportin the try". It's not that they taught me to never get firm with a horse, but they taught me to know when and how. Most important of all, they taught me to recognize the smallest try from a horse whether it is as small as a change in expression of the eye or as big as a change in the speed and direction of the feet. To use an expression from Ray Hunt, recognizing the small changes allowed me to learn to "do as much as necessary and as little as possible."

HORSES DON'T FLY- DO THEY?

One of the most important lessons I learned from Walt and Amos was the difference between making a horse do a job and allowing him to do a job. It was clear that most of us get so focused on a job that it is the job itself that becomes important.

Walt once said "Ya know matey, if ya let the horse do what he wants to do then ya aint ever gotta problem. Trainin's simple like that. But people get into trouble 'cause they don't know how to help the horse have the same ideas as them. Most folk try to impose their own idea on a horse, instead of letting their idea be the horse's idea and allowing the horse to do the job."

At the time this sounded a little "airy fairy" and really didn't mean much for awhile. But as I watched more and more people training their horses I saw them imposing their ideas on the horse. This was often accompanied by some great battles. Admittedly there was always a winner and often times it was the rider, but unfortunately there was also always a loser too. It seemed to me that Walt had been trying to teach me that there should be no losers.

There was a new girl that had been coming to the riding school almost every day. Her dad had bought her a pretty nice thoroughbred gelding that had jumped some big courses in his career and was expected to earn a room full of trophies and ribbons for his new owner. The girl was kind of pleasant on the eye, so being a normal teenage boy with normal interests I was often caught by the boss watching her on the jumping course when I should have been shoveling.

Over the coming weeks I watched the new girl work her horse nearly every day. The horse was initially prone to running out on spread fences, but with some strong riding the baulking became less and less frequent. However, this was soon followed by her horse running out through the shoulder on the turns around the course. Again, the girl was a strong enough rider to correct the problem and get her horse around the course and over the jumps. She seemed pretty happy with his progress and her ability to deal with each problem as it arose. What she wasn't so adept at handling was the way in which the horse became more difficult to catch. He was even becoming snitchy to saddle and mount. His flat work was suffering too, with lots tail swishing and an increasing level of crooked-ness in his body. All this started small, but gradually built into something that was becoming too obvious to ignore. But in the end, she decided that he was a showjumper and he was jumping with few faults and making good times, so the rest was not so much of a problem.

I was mentioning this to Walt. He had already noticed it too.

"Well matey, I guess that little horse thinks that maybe there is better things on offer when she aint around and he don't wanna be caught," Walt said. "She aint givin him the support he needs."

I pointed out that the horse was jumping pretty well.

"Maybe. But that girl aint givin the horse much choice in the jumpin, so he has to make his feelin's known in areas that he gits some choice, like bein caught. If she'd support 'im in them little things that bother him in the jump ring instead of forcin the issue, she'd get along much better."

I had to ask what did Walt really mean, since I was still not used to the way his mind and his tongue ran loops around each other.

In his usual laconic manner he replied, "That girl just forces that horse into jumpin them jumps. She aint been listen to him when he begun runnin off to the side. He needed somebody to understand that he had a problem with them jumps and who could help solve his problem by supportin and directin him to lookin at them in anotha way. But she aint figured he was anythin but stubborn or lazy and forced him to jumpin despite his worry. Now she's got to pay for it 'cause now he hates jumpin, hates ridin and hates her. He aint gonna to do anythin he don't need to. He has to jump, but sometimes he don't have to be caught or he don't have to standstill to be saddled or travel straight - so he don't."

"But Walt, can you ever get a horse to enjoy jumping? I mean I know Tolley seems to like to jump, but I've never seen him jump a fence alone when I've let him out to graze in the jumping paddock. It seems to me if a horse enjoys something he'll do it whether or not somebody is riding him. So maybe anything we do with our horses is always imposing our will at the expense of their will."

"That's an interesting question, but don't forget about supportin your horse. The reason Tolley don't jump a fence on his own is because nobody is supportin him. He needs ya to be there to make him feel he can do it and it's not a problem. If you aint there to support and encourage him, his confidence aint big enough to let him know it's ok to jump them fences. You ever notice how Burner don't ever try to avoid puddles when I ride him down the trail? I don't do nothin to make sure he goes into them puddles, he just walks straight ahead like they weren't even there. But you can bet if I weren't there to support him, and he was on his own, he'd side step every puddle."

I wasn't too sure if I agreed with Walt. It seemed like a bit of stretch to think that just being there was enough to turn something a horse didn't want to do into something he enjoyed doing. Then Walt put it into words that made human sense.

"Does it bother ya to fly in one of them big planes?"

"No, I kind of like it Walt," I replied.

"Ok. Would it bother ya if I told you the pilot couldn't make it today and just gave ya the keys and told ya to fly the plane?"

"You know it would," I said.

"Well then matey, flyin don't bother ya at all and it's even a bit of fun as long as ya get the proper support that a qualified pilot can give ya. But if I tried to force ya to fly a plane with no proper pilot we'd have one big fight on our hands. Horses ain't no different. Ya give them the support and directin they need and work can be fun for them too. But ya try forcin them into something they aint sure about and there could be trouble."

"What do you mean by support, Walt."

"Supportin a horse is preparin a horse. Ya get him ready for what is about to come, so when it comes he's prepared and it don't bother him much. I'm too old to get bucked off and I ain't been bucked by a horse in thirty years and I've been breakin them young uns for all that time. I don't get bucked 'cause I prepare them young uns before I get on them so they don't feel the need to buck when I get on. I don't try to stop 'em from bucking. I just let 'em feel it ain't important. That's supportin a horse. If I didn't support them horses, I'd have a few more broken bones by now."

"That girl ya is so fond of admirin, is not supportin her horse for them fences. She needs to prepare him better for them spreads he's so keen to avoid, instead of just forcin him over them. Any horse that is supported, prepared and directed in the right way can do anythin. Ya just set it up and let the horse get the same idea you have and he'll come through for ya every time. Ya can count on it."

Prepare your horse for the job ahead, set up the situation and let the horse do his job. It's so simple! Why do we make it so hard for our horses? How come old Walt knew this simple philosophy and the rest of us carry on oblivious to the obvious? But then if it is so simple, why do I still struggle with practicing it?

WHAT A HORSE NOTICES

Horses are amazing observers. There is not much that happens around a horse that goes unnoticed. As horse owners most of us already know this. We have either observed it ourselves or been told about it by our instructor or read about it in a book. I was told this detail of horse behaviour when I was quite young. But I didn't really understand the complexity and the depth of what that little fact really meant to me as a horse trainer.

Early on in my association with horses I had noticed that some people talked to their horses quite a lot. It seemed to be a point of great pride with some people that they were able to shout a command to their horse and elicit the response they wanted. The idea of using a voice command to work a horse fascinated me. The opportunity to try using talk to a horse as a training aid came with the arrival of a 10 year old thoroughbred gelding named Pablo to the riding school. The owner of the riding school at bought him from a trail riding establishment and had plans to turn him into a lesson horse. Pablo had not had much handling and had only been ridden a handful of times.

I started with trying to teach Pablo to walk and trot on the lunge just from my voice. I had seen several people do it before, so I figured I had a pretty good idea how to go about this project. After a few days, Pablo was getting the idea of walk and trot from just my voice. But there was a problem with getting the walk or the trot that I wanted. Sometimes he would trot fast and other times he would jog. I tried adjusting my voice and my whip to get a better result, but the outcome was always inconsistent. I began to watch other people at the riding school who used their voice a lot. Mostly, they got the same result every time. Rarely did I see their horses respond with anything but the same trot or the same walk that the horse always gave. I talked to one lady who always used her voice when riding or lunging her horse. She didn't seem to think that there was a problem as long as the horse walked, trotted or cantered when told. In fact, I'm not even sure she understood what I was talking about. I guess it was time to ask Walt about how to alter Pablo's response to my voice.

"Well matey, there ain't nothing wrong with talking to ya horse. When me and Amos was little there was a neighbour that lived a mile or two up the road and we used to hear him talkin to his horses all the time." Walt must've thought that was funny because he chuckled to himself as if it was the funniest joke he had heard in a long time.

"I think the answer to ya question is in the paddock. Spend a bit of time watchin Pablo and his mates talkin to each other and ya'll probably see why ya gotta a problem.

This is why I had come to Walt with some reluctance. He rarely gave a straight answer. He was like the school teacher who would use a big word, then tell you to go to the library to look up the meaning. All I wanted was an answer and Walt turned it into homework. I decided that I didn't want to know the answer so badly that I would spend hours sitting around the paddock, but I would keep an occasional eye on activities in Pablo's paddock and see what I would see.

Over several days I paid some attention to what was going on in the paddock. I saw horses getting moved by other horses to free up a shady spot or to gain access to the water trough. I saw mutual grooming parties. I saw the herd relax while at least one member stood guard. I saw occasional playful spurts of exuberance that entailed some galloping, a few bucks and some head to head rearing by a couple of horses. But I didn't see much at all that gave me the secret to how to get a horse more responsive to my voice. So I finally went back to Walt.

"Well matey, ya told me what ya did see. But what didn't ya see?"

"Walt, how can I tell you about something that I didn't see happen? That doesn't make sense."

"Matey, ya didn't see too many horses makin a lot of chatter in the paddock did ya? Did ya hear one horse whiny to another to move along? Did ya hear a horse tell another horse that he wanted his wither scratched? Did ya hear them horses discuss who was going to stay on guard while the rest of them slept?"

"Matey, the reason that Pablo ain't real good in his responses to ya voice commands is 'cause horses ain't real good at talkin or listenin to sounds. I read somewhere that them scientific blokes reckon that horses have only nine sounds that horses make. If that's true then horses can't rely on their voices to communicate a lot to other horses. It's not their way. It's not how Mother Nature made them. So when we humans start tryin to teach them our way of communicatin it don't work too good. There ain't nothin wrong with usin ya voice. But just be aware how limitin it is when ya need to communicate a lot of information to a horse. Now lets go and have a look at Pablo and I'll show ya somethin that might be more useful to ya."

I went and got Pablo from his paddock. Walt said to bring him over to the arena with just a halter and long rope. When I got there Walt took Pablo and asked him to circle out from him. I watched Walt take him through his paces. Pablo walked, trotted and cantered. He changed direction. Then when that was all looking good I watched Walt get Pablo to walk fast, then slow. He got Pablo to trot out at a nice even pace. Then he got him to extend the length of his stride without changing his rhythm. Walt asked Pablo to quicken his trot without lengthening. Pablo made all these changes with hardly any discernible effort. But was more amazing was that I couldn't see how Walt was doing it. Walt didn't utter one sound, nor did he seem to make much change in himself to get the changes in Pablo. I watched Walt as closely and as carefully as I could, but still didn't see what he was doing to cause Pablo to respond. Eventually, I just gave up trying to work it out and asked Walt what he was doing.

"Well matey, I'm changin meself. Watch me breathin when I want Pablo to trot and walk."

I still couldn't see what Walt wanted me to see and I told him so.

"When I want Pablo to trot I prepare him by increasin my rate of breathin. I make it a bit quicker and a tad more shallow. When I want him to walk, I let out a lot of air. He sees it all and responds the way I want."

I told Walt I didn't know a horse could be that sensitive and observant.

"Sight and smell are the horse's main tools of communication. Ya notice how they are always smellin things - people, dogs, saddles, a rag on the ground, poo on the trail. Well matey, there is lot of information in those smells for a horse. He can tell a lot about his world from those smells. I reckon that's how a horse tells the difference between men and women. I reckon they smell the difference."

"But the other way a horse reads about his world is by watchin. Pablo can tell when my breathin changes. Now he's more sensitive than a lot, because he ain't been handled so much that he has learned to ignore most things a human does with their body. But ya can teach a horse to be real responsive to such small changes in ya body that ya would think they were readin ya thoughts. Trouble is that most people use big and exaggerated movements. We swing our arms around, we kick with our legs, we throw our weight from side to side. All this information can get too much for a horse if he don't learn to ignore a lot of it. Horses can sorta filter out a lot of information if they need to. That's how ya turn a responsive horse into a dull horse. Do so much with ya body actions that they are forced to learn to ignore most of what ya do. I reckon that's why so many people have real problems with Arabs. Arabs are so smart and sensitive that they find it hard to cope with people who can't control the way they use themselves. Arabs find it hard to filter out what is important and what isn't when a person is movin around them, so they get confused, worried and in a whole lot of trouble."

"It takes a lot of practice and skill for us dumb humans to learn to control our bodies because we think the only way to communicate is with the voice. So we try to teach our horses to perform to our voice. But it don't work too good when ya want somethin more than the most simple changes in a horse. There ain't nothin wrong with usin the voice if ya only want simple things from a horse, but sooner or later most of us have to learn the subtleties of communicatin in their language - the body language. If an untrained fellow like Pablo can give to me when I only slightly change me breathin, think what he could do when he is trained. Maybe I could get him to give when I only think about changing me breathin!"

FLOAT LOADING THROUGH FEEL

Growing up in the northern suburbs of Sydney made it impossible for me to have a horse of my own. Working at the riding school was the only way that I could be around horses and ride. It started when I was very young with shoveling out stables in return for a riding lesson. I was almost too young to drive the wheel barrow and certainly too young to negotiate the barrow up the steep, narrow boards that led to the top of the manure heap. More than once I lost my load before getting to the top. But eventually I graduated to more glamorous jobs like cleaning saddles, feeding horses and even giving lessons! By the time I was in my early teens I was teaching more and more and had an itch to compete. I didn't own a horse of my own and so relied on the generosity of people who did own horses. I had broken in a few horses and had been helping Walt and Amos with some of their projects. I think people reckoned that if I was good enough to be working with the two old brothers, then I was good enough to handle and ride their horses.

One of the horses that I had the pleasure to ride at competitions in the very early days was a horse called Chelsea. I had taken her into a few hack classes, but my passion (and hers) was jumping. Her owner was happy for me to take Chelsea to local gymkhanas and liked it even more when we came home decorated with ribbons. When I started working with Chelsea she was a reluctant float loader. She would often stop at the bottom of the ramp or run around the side. I knew that this needed to be fixed if I was going to be taking Chelsea to shows regularly. I knew Chelsea was a food hog and started working on her float loading problem with a biscuit of hay in the front. Within a few days Chelsea was virtually running into the back of the float almost before the ramp was all the way down. I was really pleased with how well she had progressed with her loading problem and felt we were ready to go anywhere.

Shortly after this the owner and I took Chelsea to a show for the day. There was no problem getting her on the float and she seemed to travel well. When we got there Chelsea unloaded like an angel and we went about getting ready for the events. The day was a mixed bag of success and no success, but we had fun anyway. The owner appeared to be pretty happy with Chelsea and even managed to shrug off some of the errors I made around the jump course. When it came time to go home, Chelsea got stuck about going into the float. Only a few hours prior she practically ran into the float of her own accord, but now she was standing at the ramp refusing to budge. I couldn't understand what went wrong. There was hay in the front - lucerne - her favourite. After several tries I finally asked the owner to get behind her and give her a whack on the rump with a lead rope. She leapt into the float and stood quietly while we locked the ramp.

A few days after this show I decided I needed to do more float training with Chelsea. I got somebody to hook up their car to Chelsea's float. I was expecting a bit of a struggle from Chelsea and was ready for it, but it didn't happen. Chelsea just barreled straight into the back of the float like she had done before. Mmmm! Maybe the other day was just an aberration and wouldn't happen again. But I was wrong. On three successive outings to shows Chelsea was fine to load in the morning, but refused to load for the trip home. Then when I was getting ready to go to a show one Saturday morning, Chelsea refused to load again. This was now becoming a more serious problem and I didn't know why. I figured it was time to call in the big guns and I went in search of Walt and Amos for some advice.

I interrupted the old men sitting under a tree. There were sipping tea poured from a beat up thermos and munching on ANZAC biscuits while their horses milled around listening to their conversation. They asked what was up and I explained the problem I was having with Chelsea. But they were in no hurry to help and poured me a cuppa while I waited for them to finish morning smoko. Finally Walt said to Amos, "Well, I guess I might as well go over and see what this young fella was beatin up on his horse for."

Walt wandered over where Chelsea and her owner were waiting for us by the float. I explained to Walt what had been happening. I tried to load Chelsea, but she stopped again. I started to give her ever increasing taps with a whip before she finally scooted into the float. She had a munch on the hay and then I unloaded her. I began to ask her to go in again and she immediately hopped into the float. I repeated the exercise again, but this time Chelsea started into the float before I asked. I thought this all looked pretty good and turned to see what Walt thought.

"Well matey, what do you think is goin on here," he asked?

"Well, Walt she looks like she is pretty keen to get into the float. This is what she was like before, but then I started having problems again. Why do you reckon she can be good sometimes and then jack up about loading on other times?"

'Well ya see matey, she ain't ever gone into that float because ya asked her. She's just goin in because she wants to. Sometimes she wants to and sometimes she don't. She's probably jumpin in there because she's got her mind fixed on gettin to that hay. But at the times when she ain't interested in hay or more interested in other stuff, she ain't got it in her head to go in the float. Ya ain't never got her followin your feel. She's just doin her own thing. It just so happens that half the time her thing is loadin up and you think that's a pretty good deal because that's what your thing is too."

"So Walt, you're saying that even when she is loading into the float, she's not listening to me. She is more likely listening to her stomach. And when her stomach isn't telling her to go into the float, that's when I have the trouble?"

"That's right matey," he responded.

"What do I do? Do I take out the hay," I asked?

"Well ya could, but I don't think that's going to make much difference. See how she jumps and rushes into the float. Get rid of that. Instead

127

of lettin her rush in, allow her to only go in one foot at a time. At first she'll try to push past ya and rush. Stop her and shut her down. Let her settle there. Then ask for another step. Then another. If she tries to go more than one foot at a time, stop her and back her out one foot. Get her to feel of ya and her mind on ya instead of that hay. Ya oughta be able to get her to go in as far as ya like and stop her anywhere ya like, anytime ya like. If ya can get that workin at that sorta of level you've actually achieved somethin worthwhile. It comes down to whether or not she's followin ya feel or workin on auto pilot. If she's workin on auto pilot, there'll be a time when the auto is switched off and ya won't get the job done. But if she's followin ya feel, you'll get her loaded every time."

I had heard Walt and Amos talk about following a feel hundreds of times before. I thought I always knew what they were talking about, but at this moment a new light bulb switched on for me. I finally saw a concrete example of why "following a feel" was important. It was a turning point for me in my understanding of training horses. Over a long time I began to learn about "following a feel" with whatever I was doing around a horse. I learned ways of applying it when I had a horse at the end of a lead rope and when I was doing a dressage test. It became useful when I was saddling up and when I was setting up for a jump. I tried teaching it when I was grooming a horse and when I was teaching him to lay down on command. I have since learned to always be teaching the idea of "following my feel" to every horse I touch and every time I touch it. "Following a feel" has since become important in everything I do with horses. I don't always have horses long enough to get it truly established, but I still strive for it and have learned how much safer, reliable and enjoyable it is to be around horses when the feel is there.

WHAT CAN A CHICKEN
TEACH YOU ABOUT A HORSE?

This may sound a pretty stupid question. It seems hardly likely that chickens have anything to teach us about horses. But I learned long ago that you can learn the most insightful lessons about horse behaviour from the most unexpected sources. I often think horses have a lot in common with young children. They sometimes share the same motivations and even reactions under certain circumstances. But a little while ago I was reminded of something that I learned about horses when I was a young fellow and it had to do with chickens. I guess I should start the story with what happened to bring back these memories.

My friend Margo bought a really nice thoroughbred gelding a few months ago. Things had been going pretty well and they looked a fairly impressive combination. That is until I got a phone call. It seems there was a disagreement between Margo and her latest gold medal prospect. Wilt is not the sort of horse who likes to stand around arguing all day, so he decided to resolve the dispute quickly by rearing and dumping my friend on her backside. Apparently this was not the first disagreement they had had, but my friend had become sick and tired of the way that Wilt kept settling their disputes. Margo called me up to ask me to act as an independent arbitrator in this matter We made a time for me to drop by and listen to both sides.

On arrival, I saw Margo getting ready to ride Wilt in a smallish cleared patch in the paddock. There were no fences or defined perimeter in the working area. She walked him around and he was ok, except I noticed he would always drop the outside shoulder in a couple of the corners. When Wilt trotted, this got worse and Margo was using a lot of inside rein and outside leg to get him to make the turn. It seemed to me that rather than just a balance problem, Wilt was trying to escape the arena through the corners on that side of the arena. I asked Margo about this and she said that the trouble always started on those corners and when he got bad he would prop himself and rear against the inside rein. Bingo! A light bulb went on straight away. That side of the work area was closest to the gate. Good 'ol Wilt was trying to go home via the gate. He was what trainers call gate bound or barn sour. All he wanted was to go home through the gate and he was getting cranky when Margo insisted he go past the gate.

I understood Margo's frustration. I'd been there when I was a young fellow. I remember

Walt teaching me about chickens. For a short time at the riding school it was my job every evening to round the chooks up in their large pen and get them into the small chook shed and safe from foxes at night. Every time it was a job and a half. Those chooks would scatter everywhere as I tried to herd them. Just when I thought they were going through the door of the shed they'd scatter like confetti at a wedding.

"I bet if there was a fox around, those chooks would run into that shed quick smart," Walt
said to me when I went over to ask him for some help. "Why don't you make like a fox?"

Walt chortled as he walked away to the big shed.

I couldn't work out what he meant at first. Did he want me to get on all fours and wear a fox skin? It took me a few days and more frustration to sort out in my mind what Walt was trying to tell me. Finally I figured it out. The chooks would run into the shed because with the fox around they didn't want to be outside. I reckon Walt was trying to tell me that instead of trying to force them into the shed, all I had to do was make it so the chooks didn't want to be out in the pen. I got the idea of using my kelpie to pace the perimeter of the pen. This made the chooks a little nervous and it wasn't long before those brainless birds got the idea pretty quick. It only took a couple of weeks for the chickens to learn to automatically wander into the pen when they saw me coming towards them at the end of the day.

These thoughts passed through my mind as I watched Margo struggle with Wilt. It seemed to me Wilt wanted to go to the gate and Margo wanted Wilt to stay away from the gate. If she got Wilt to change his mind about the gate being a good place to go, she wouldn't have to argue with him. All she had to do was make it so Wilt didn't want to go to the gate and he would be happy to stay in the arena. Getting into a fight with Wilt was what was getting Margo into trouble. On the other hand, if she stayed on the right side of trouble but still made Wilt think the gate was not a pleasant place to be, she'd sort it out.

We started by getting Margo to walk Wilt around the arena and letting go of the reins. Of course, Wilt headed towards the gate. When he got within about 8 metres of the gate I told her to vibrate her lower legs in an alternate fashion (left leg, then right leg, then left leg). I didn't want her to kick him, just niggle him with her leg and to leave the reins alone. Wilt was allowed to go anywhere he wanted. Wherever he went was going to be his choice and not somebody else steering him to go somewhere. At first Wilt hurried to the gate, but when he got there I had Margo continue to niggle him. He moved around a lot at the gate looking for somewhere to go. Margo's legs were uncomfortable enough for him to not be able to stand still at the gate, but not so uncomfortable that he needed to bolt off somewhere. She gave him just enough pressure to keep him searching for a way out of his situation. He paced back and forth across the gate for a minute of so. Finally he looked as if he thought of leaving the gate and I had Margo keep her legs quiet and relaxed. Immediately he went back to the gate and again Margo used her legs and no reins.

In a few moments, Wilt turned away from the gate and Margo stopped using her legs. He walked about 3 metres before turning back to the gate. Again, Margo used her legs. This time he walked passed the gate and circled away for a much bigger trip. Soon, he headed back to the gate and Margo started to vibrate her legs. Wilt instantly turned away from the gate and headed back out towards the middle of the paddock. There were a few more attempts to return to the gate, but every time Margo was there to annoy him with her legs when he tried. Within 30 minutes Wilt was making trips all over the paddock with no thought of returning to the gate on his own.

It took another 3 or 4 sessions before Wilt became reliably cured of his gate bound behaviour. It became reliable because Margo let Wilt discover that he didn't want to go to the gate, rather than trying to forcibly steer him away from the gate each time he came pass. This way she allowed her idea to become Wilts idea and instead of arguing over whose idea to follow they both agreed that going past the gate was a good idea. I think that's just how Walt would have done it too.

IS IT TOO MUCH TROUBLE
TO BOTHER A HORSE?

Horses are constantly reminding me just how little I know about them. Sometimes I get a run of horses for training and things go pretty well. I get a little cocky and start to think that maybe I really know what I'm doing. That's when you can be sure that somebody will send me a horse that will test me to the limit of my skills. When I get a tough case sometimes I'm left wondering if I really did as good a job as possible. I don't back away from those tough horses because I reckon each one gives me a chance to learn something new or to get better in one area of horsemanship that I don't get much practice. But these horses keep me awake at night because my brain is spinning so fast searching for answers on how best to help them.

One of the first horses I ever got to work on my own was a very sensitive Arab mare. I was fifteen at the time and had been hanging around Walt and Amos for a few years. Amos knew the owner and it was his suggestion that she ask me to re-train her horse. I took this as a great honour and vote of confidence from my mentors. Amos and his older twin brother Walt were ancient. They had ancient faces and ancient bones and moved with the speed of a one-legged tortoise. But their brains and their feeling for horses was what made them special. They were a gold mine of knowledge when it came to horses. They generally kept to themselves and were considered just eccentric old men by most people. But I was lucky. They liked that I had a passion for horses and a thirst for understanding and helping troubled horses. I became their apprentice and they were my de facto professors.

The Arab was a worried little thing. She would run around the round yard as fast as she liked, bashing the rails as she went. She wasn't really running from anything, she was just running. She would do this even if nobody was in the round yard or nearby. For the first few days I just watched her and didn't really introduce myself other than to give her a pat if she approached me. I would watch her in the paddock or the yard and try to work out what she was always running from.

When I did get around to putting some work into her, I decided that I needed to go slow and steady and just keep reassuring her that I was not the monster she should run from. I put her on the end of a lead rope and taught her to disengage her hindquarters, then to yield her forehand across to the feel of the rope. I worked on getting her to back up and taught her to come forward. Being as Arabs are generally so smart, she caught on to this stuff very quickly. The slightest lifting of the lead rope caused her front feet to follow the ropes direction. She was so soft - it was a beautiful thing to feel. I constantly patted her and tried to sooth her nervousness. But despite her softness and despite my care not to scare or frazzle her, she continued to live as if a horse-eating monster was about to jump at her anytime.

Nearly three weeks had passed since I first began working the little mare. I was getting frustrated because although she was becoming very polite and very obedient and very soft, she was still a bundle of nerves inside. It seemed that I was making changes on the outside of the horse, but not on the inside. Little things would still cause her to spook. When I asked her to do something it had to be only the quietest, softest request otherwise she would freak out. It was difficult to be casual around her for fear of frightening her. I didn't understand why she was not getting calmer.

I knew Walt and Amos had been keeping a distant eye on everything I did with the mare. They had not offered any advice or made any comment. That was not their way. They knew that the best time to give advice is when it is requested. Well, it was that time. I needed help and I knew who to ask.

"Well matey, it seems to me she ain't sure about anythin," Amos told me. "She's so busy lookin 'round for anythin that might scare her that she'd don't even know that you and her go together."

I didn't understand what Amos was talking about and asked for clarification.

"She's always lookin for something to scare her. When a bird flies from one of them gums, she gets scared 'cause she ain't know'd it was there. When ya ask her to do somethin, she thinks ya is one of them birds and gets scared 'cause she don't even know ya was there. Her mind is like one them birds. It flies 'round all over lookin for somethin to land on and never stays lookin at the same thing for more than a second or two."

"But why, Amos?"

"Because she aint got any confidence. She don't know what's important for her to focus on to stay alive, so she looks at anythin that may look scary in case she misses the monster she knows is out there to get her. She ain't like that black pony in the other paddock that's afraid of people and needs some gentlin. She's afraid of her surroundins and what is out there."

"Ok Amos, how do I fix it," I asked?

"Tomorrow we'll have a lessin in the mornin."

When I got there the next day, Amos already had the mare in the round yard and was trying to get a saddle on her. Whenever he presented the saddle to her she stepped her hindquarters away from him.

"Did ya see that, matey? She done moved her end away and she ain't even lookin at me. Her mind is outside this yard. I'm goin to change that for her."

When Amos approached her again with the saddle she moved her rear end away. Amos walked another step towards her and asked her to stay with the end of the lead rope. The mare hardly took any notice and kept moving away. What happened next caught me by surprise. Amos gave an almighty flick down the lead rope which caught the mare under the chin with a loud "thwack" (this is why Amos never used a clip to secure the lead rope to the halter). The mare leapt backwards in shock and froze staring at Amos. I thought I had just seen all my work of trying to gentle this mare, go down the drain. Amos walked up to the mare and petted her forehead and neck, then asked her to walk forward. He stopped her and asked her to stand still while he put the saddle over her back. She never moved and stayed looking at him.

The session continued in much the same way. Every time the mare lost concentration on Amos, he would ask her politely to check him out again. If she ignored his request a quick flick of that lead rope reminded her that he was more important in her life than anything else. Pretty soon the mare could stand quietly and relaxed for saddling. Amos did lots of work with her in that short session and she softened and lost a lot of her nervousness.

"Ya see matey, I became so importin to the mare that she didn't have to worry about anythin else that was goin on 'round her. As long as she knew where I was she could cope with the stress of every day life."

"But Amos, why wasn't she more scared when you flicked her with the rope? How come she started to relax after a bit much better than all the time I spent being gentle and quiet with her?"

"See matey, she got secure in knowin that as long as she stayed with me and kept lookin me up, life would be ok. A horse ain't bothered by bein scared. They spend their whole life being scared of things every day. They get scared, comfortable, then scared, then comfortable again and that don't bother them too much. She can get over the things that scare her. Bein bothered by stuff becomes her way of livin. You might show her a different way of handlin bein scared and show her she don't need to jump out of skin every time somethin scares her. But she'll be bothered by things just the same.. What I done this mornin is let her know that if she's bothered by stuff, life is better if she stays listnin to me. She can get real secure with that thought and things ain't likely to bother her nearly so much."

"A little botherin is no trouble to a horse if she knows a way out of the bother. If she is scared, show her a way out of being scared and she'll not be bothered. She'll learn to trust in ya. Where people get into trouble is they turn a little botherin into trouble by not settin it up that shows a horse a way out of her bother. She then gets to thinkin her life is in danger and next thing ya know you got a whole storm brewin inside of that mare. It's hard to ride a storm."

What Amos was telling me proved to be profound. There is nothing wrong with a horse getting scared. Being scared and insecure is a way of life for horses. That's why they are first and foremost animals of flight. But what Amos was saying was that if you do get your horse scared make sure of two things. First, don't allow something that worries a horse become something that terrifies a horse. You do this by not over facing a horse into a situation that it is too difficult to handle for her. This is best done by making sure there is a way out of the worry that the horse can find fairly easily. The second criteria is to ensure you never leave the horse in the worried state. Make sure she comes out the other side of the fear in a more relaxed frame of mind.

The majority of worried or scared horses need to be handled with gentleness. But in the case of the little Arab filly, Amos could see that her problem lay in a lack of focus on me. He surmised that she got frightened because she felt all on her own. She didn't have the confidence to look to me for help so she generally ignored me so she could keep a watchful focus on everything around her that may jump out and scare her. Amos worked out that if he gave her enough reason to keep her focus on him, she would begin to ignore most of the things around that bothered her. Again, I should stress that this is not something you would do with every nervous horse. There are only some horses out there with whom you may want to take this type of approach.

"Amos, how did you know that it was ok to flick the mare with the rope," I asked?

"She done told me. I had thought that it might help, so I asked her. She then came back with the fact that it did. I might have been wrong and she'd have come back with the fact that my opinion was wrong. Then I'd have had to make anotha opinion. She knew what was the truth. She always will. I only have the opinions, she has the facts. That's the way it always is, matey.

GREAT HORSEMAN

When I was a kid I was an avid reader of all books concerned with riding and horsemanship. Later on I made a point of studying the ways of as many horsemen I could find. It was and is an obsession of mine. One of the things that always interested me was not only the similarities between the best riders and trainer, but the difference as well. I started to wonder if it was possible for two people to ride and train horses very differently and still be equally great horse people? As I got older and learned more of the wisdom of Walt and Amos I began to understand that truly great horse people don't subscribe to methods or a system because they had learned the importance of 'feel' and what it means to work with the inside of the horse. They are people who understand the restrictions and limitations of a structured system when it comes to educating horses. The best horse people have a philosophy that does not waiver, but they have ways of doing things that waiver all the time – from horse to horse and moment to moment.

With this discovery I thought I had found the secret to becoming a truly great horseman. I figured that as my 'feel' and timing improved I was on the way to becoming as good a horseman as the best of them – including Walt and Amos. Alas, this was not true. My skills did improve and my ability to handle the more difficult horses was steadily growing. In fact, I got quite a bit of work from people who had heard how I fixed so-and-so's horse problem or how good a job I had done breaking in a horse for some people whose daughter went to school with their girl. I liked the work. I really liked the money and I also like the notoriety. It got to the stage that I figured that Walt, Amos and I were like the three amigos. Looking back on it, I realize how foolish and stupid I was. But mixing my age and experience at the time with a little bit of ego and flattery from others and you get a stupid, foolish teenager.

Fortunately reality did not come as a rude crashing to earth for me. I didn't embarrass myself in a way that would traumatize me for life and have me living in a cave by myself for the rest of my days. Rather it came from wanting to be like Walt and Amos. Spending as much time as I could with these two old men taught me that not only were they able to train horses for any task that was required, but they were also able to achieve a friendship and mutual respect with their horses. This showed itself in ways that were only visible if you looked carefully for them. The way a timid and nervous horse got braver and calmer under the tutelage of the brothers. The sour horse that was always snitchy when asked to go forward would soften his thoughts when guided by the old men. The horses that had fear of people would melt to the touch of Walt or Amos. I wanted to know the secrets to these things. What made these cranky and wizen old men from a generation that thought talking films were wondrous, not just horse educators but horse therapists? I wanted to know.

"Amos, what do you reckon you need to have to be a really good horse person," I asked?

"Well matey, I ain't had time to think about it. You ask a hard question there. I guess you need lots of things."

"Well Amos, what do you think is the most important thing?"

"Well matey, let me ask you somethin. That pony that ya was workin for that lady last week. Did ya like him?"

"Yeah, he was a nice horse. Nothing special, but polite and had a try in him once I showed him that "no" was not the right answer," I said.

"How did ya know that "no" was not the right answer, matey?"

"What do you mean, Amos? Of course he had to learn that he had to go into the float. That's what he was here for," I said.

"Yep matey, that's what he was here for. But do ya know the difference between a good horse trainer and a great horse trainer?"

"What," I asked?

"You take Walt as an example, matey. Do ya know why he is about the best horsemen ya ever goin to see in ya life? No, of course ya don't. Ya don't know enough yet. The secret is that he don't think he is any better than any horse. He respects 'em in a way you or I or anybody around here can never understand. Walt don't put 'imself above any horse. When he works with a horse he's workin with a friend on the same footin. He ain't treatin 'em like a dumb animal. Walt believes with all his heart that every horse is just as smart, just as good and just as deservin of the same respect as he is. It ain't just words for him – he knows it's true. That's why he is so good with horses, matey."

"But Amos, don't ya need to be a leader and make the right thing real easy and the wrong thing more difficult? I mean that's what you and Walt have taught me."

"Sure matey. A horse needs leadership and how to get along with people that's safe and proper for both. But matey, if I was to teach ya how to play chess would it be right for me to think I'm better than ya because I know the rules and you don't? I wouldn't be better than ya and a person ain't better than a horse just 'cause the horse don't know how to go on the float.

And ya know what matey? If I respected ya as an equal do ya think I would be a better teacher than if I tried to show ya how to play chess with me actin all superior and smug? What Walt has in his heart with how he feels about horses gives him somethin that the rest of us won't ever get by just practicin to ride and train them. He has an advantage that ya can only get by makin changes to how ya feel. That's pretty special."

"Amos are you telling me that Walt is a better horseman than you?"

"Maybe matey, but I ain't jealous because I got all the good looks in the family."

What Amos had to say gave me a lot to think about. It got me re-evaluating how I had approached the problem with the pony. It later occurred to me that maybe I should get Walt's input on what elements go into making somebody a great horse person.

"Well matey, there's a whole lot of things that are important if ya is to become the best ya can be. But ya know what I reckon sets the good from the great? Ya gotta love them. Ya gotta love horses."

"Well I think most of us love horses, Walt. Otherwise we would be riding bikes," I observed.

"No matey. Most of us only love horses with conditions attached. Most of us love horses 'cause we love to ride or they are so beautiful or they win ribbons for us or we love the feelin of being in control of somethin so big and strong. Not too many folk love horse for what they are. Who loves the ugliest horse in the country or who loves the horse that attacks them when they walk into the paddock or the horse that nobody else wants? The sort of love that comes from inside a person because that's the sort of person they are. It's rare to find. That's why Amos is better with any horse you'll ever see. He loves them for what they are. He don't care much about what they can do or will do or look like. He loves them with no conditions. Every damn one of them! And somehow, in a way that I ain't ever understood, they know it and he gets somethin special from them. I guess it's because the role he takes in their life is a leadership they understand best. I don't know how a horse would explain it, but I reckon it is somethin like for us a parent would act. Ya mum and dad matey love ya with no conditions and ya know it. This makes their role in ya life special above anybody else. Ya respond and respect them in a way that is different from the way ya are with anybody else. That's how it is for Amos and the horses. He's got all the skills, the awareness, the timin, the feel and all the things they other good horse people have, but he's also got this special love for them which makes the results you and I get look ordinary. But ya know matey, I don't mind too much because when the ladies are around it's usually me they have got their eye on. Poor Amos got stuck with his ugly mug, so I figure he and I are about even in life's luck."

I walked away stunned. Did each brother know how much respect the other had for them? I had never heard anything but jibs from one about the other. But here they were expressing their awe at the others horse skills! But what was even clearer was their observation that apart from the obvious technical skills that a person needs to have to be good with horses, there was an inner love and respect for all horses that one needs in order to be the best you can.

And what about humility? Each brother recognized something special in the other, but didn't see it in themselves. They each described a deep love and respect for the horse. But to have such an inner feeling for horses must require a high degree of humility in the person. How humble must a person be to not put themselves above a horse? I have only seen this in maybe one or two other people in my life. It's a very rare gift. How does one achieve such humility? This was something that was missing from my understanding. I have no idea if I am getting any better with this aspect of horsemanship. I find at times I have to remind myself to be respectful and love the horse for what he is, which I guess means I have more work to do.

Finally, the other major observation I made from my conversation with the two brothers is that they were not perfect – they did get some things wrong. There was no argument that I was the best looking fellow on the place!

HOW WE INFLUENCE
OUR HORSES LIVES

Not too long ago I was sitting in the gallery of an indoor arena, along with about 25 other people, watching a well known clinician practicing his craft to an enthusiastic crowd. He was lecturing us all on the psychology of horses and the reasons for bad behaviour. At the start of his talk he made the statements that just about all of our problems with a horse's behaviour are caused by people. Which at the time I thought was fair enough – I couldn't argue with that. But he then went on to say, "you never see a horse in the paddock with a problem until somebody goes into that paddock." I thought about that a little and while I agree that people are mostly the root cause of problems we have with horses his last statement assumes that once we put our horses back in their paddock and walk away their problems are over. I was not too sure I agreed with that assumption. Experience has taught me that we can have a strong influence on a horse's behaviour even when we are not there. Let me relate two stories to illustrate what I mean.

The first comes from a friend called Len. He is a trainer and one of the handiest horseman you will see anywhere. Len had a horse called Bo who was a big strong Quarterhorse gelding. Bo was given to Len as a green, know-nothing prospect for Len to train and use as a working horse. A working horse is a horse that a trainer or clinician would ride while working other horses. They are used to drive horses around a round yard or arena. They are also used for close in work where you might dally a lead rope around the saddle horn and teach a young horse to lead, yield his hindquarters and forehand, carry a rider for the first time etc. By necessity a working horse needs to be strong and brave in his work because the horse being trained might rear or buck, kick at them, charge at them, and a stud might try to mount them and so on. The working (or saddle) horse must be able to stand his ground and even push against any aggressive behaviour that the young horse might offer.

When Len got Bo he needed a lot of basic education. He wasn't a terribly assertive horse and was always at the bottom of the pecking order of Len's herd of horses. As Bo progressed in his understanding of the basics Len began putting him to work moving young horses around the round pen during clinics. It was clear from the start that Bo was nervous of getting too close to the other horses. He would hold back from getting in too close and was only really comfortable when the horse was moving away from him. For quite awhile Len only worked Bo on stock that was easy to move in order to develop Bo's confidence. This was going pretty well and bit by bit as the months passed Bo was getting braver and began working more tough minded horses. He was learning that he could move the feet of the other horses and more often than not they would yield to his space rather than the other way around.

Len was telling me that as Bo's ability as a saddle horse was building so was his behaviour in the herd changing. Bo was starting to assert himself in the herd. He was climbing the ladder of seniority and was now second in charge. This was a real turn around from the timid gelding that was chased off by anything that came within twenty feet of him. But what surprised Len even more was that Bo seemed to have developed a mean streak. He had always been so placid in the paddock and was always the first to try to make friends with any new horse – as if he was desperate to find anybody who would be his friend. But lately Bo was greeting any new horse by charging them with all guns blazing, and he was taking no prisoners. He was chasing horses around and hassling them until he was either too tired or too bored with this game. Len believes that by training Bo as a working horse he had taught him that he had the ability to move horses rather than the other way around. Bo seemed to have taken this new found confidence into his everyday life in the paddock and learned that even without Len on his back he could move horses and take care of any situation that might arise before it did arise. He was establishing himself as senior member of the herd and nobody was going to mess with him. Bo had taken what he learned with Len and put it to work for him in other aspects of his life that had nothing to do with being a working horse for Len.

I think this story is one example of how the time spent with us can influence the way a horse can be even when we are not there. Another example comes to mind from my younger days spent around Walt and Amos.

Nancy was a new boarder who had a seven year old thoroughbred mare called Tia. The horse had raced for about four years and been given to Nancy by a family friend who wanted to retire the horse from racing. Nancy had had many horses in her life and was a pretty successful show rider. Nancy thought that Tia might become her next serious competition horse – she certainly had the looks and despite all those years of racing she had very clean legs.

Tia seemed a little hot and always came into the arena on her toes. She was unsettled in the paddock too. Every time a horse was moved from one paddock to another or was walked down a laneway, Tia would call and run the fence line of her yard. She kept tabs on everything that happened on the place and reacted in a way that reminded me of "chicken little" when the sky was falling. Like Nancy, I assumed that this was because she was a thoroughbred. They have the reputation for being "hot" and Tia was just being true to her breed – or so I thought.

It was probably a year and a half that Nancy had been agisting at the riding school when she approached me about riding her horse. She and her husband were going away for eight weeks and Nancy did not want Tia out of work for so long because she thought she would be a handful after that long without work. She also wanted her ridden to keep her muscles development looking good for the coming show season. I agreed to help her after we came to a satisfactory financial arrangement.

When I first began riding Tia I found her stiff and resistant to the reins and over reactive to the legs. Her focus was non-existent and her mind shot around the arena like a pin ball. It was difficult to keep tabs on her thoughts. Her mind was so quick and frazzled. I spent a lot of time on the ground trying to get her to let go of her tension and keep her thoughts on simple things. I know it was not what Nancy had in mind when she asked me to work her horse, but I was doing this for Tia, not Nancy.

I enlisted the help of Walt when it came to the ridden work. He gave me some pointers on how to help Tia let go of her worries and find another way to feel about me and work. About four weeks into my time with Tia I was noticing she was getting less reactive to the legs and more responsive – she was less rushy, but still nicely forward. She was softening through her body and was letting go of the tightness in the muscles of her back.

I was talking to Walt about how she was making some changes. He seemed to agree and then asked me a question.

"What's she been like to catch, matey?"

"Fine, Walt. No problem after the first few days," I replied.

"Ya noticed how little she calls now," he asked?

"Yeah, she does seem more settled," I said. "She doesn't run as much as she use to either I reckon."

"Why do ya think that is, matey?"

"I dunno know, Walt," I answered.

"Well matey, I think she ain't as confused and lost as she was a few weeks ago."

"Yeah, maybe she is doing better in her work. But I only work for an hour or so a few days a week. She spends almost all day in the paddock. She has plenty of time to get herself in a state between our rides," I said.

"Well matey, it would be a mistake to under estimate the influence that one hours work has on the rest of a horse's day. If ya leave a horse confused and upset and put him back in the paddock, he carries that feelin back to the paddock with him. That mare weren't born to be that crazy in the paddock. She's like that 'cause people upset her day almost every day of her life."

"But Walt, I thought horse's live in the moment and don't hold onto things," I said.

"To some extent matey that's true. A horse's thoughts do live in the moment. His mind flitters from one experience to another and they don't hold onto their thoughts too long. But his feelins is something different. He can't change the way he feels from one second to another without consequences. If somebody upsets ya, ya can't just turn that feelin off anytime. Ya carry that upset with ya for a while no matter what else ya might be doin. If that upset becomes part of ya every day, pretty soon if affects ya whole day. If a bully is pickin on ya at school and this happens day after day, it won't be long before ya folks notice ya behaviour changin at home. The same goes for a horse. If ya leave a horse tight and upset time after time, he will carry that with him even when ya ain't around. It will affect how he is on his own and with other horses. There is hardly anythin crueller in my book than to leave a horse mentally confused and emotionally upset.

The reason why that mare is runnin less and callin less is because ya clearin up a whole lot of confusion and worry for her about what ya is expectin from her. She's goin back to the paddock with less stress and worry in her and that feelin is holdin for a little while. If ya could keep it up, one day it will hold all day, every day."

It gave me a lot to think about. When Nancy returned from holidays she took over the training of Tia. She was very complimentary to me about how much better Tia was working, but within two or three days the stiffness and resistance came back. The running and calling in the pad-dock came back too!

We talk about cruelty in terms of physical neglect, starvation etc. but I believe horses can suffer from emotional cruelty as well. In my job I see so many horses that are lost and confused in regard to what is expect from them when being worked. This leaves such a bad feeling inside that they can carry that feeling through their whole lives. They seek comfort and can't find any. It is a terribly sad plight. If you leave a horse feeling okay inside instead of bothered, you are going a long way to making it a better life for him even when you are not there.

THE TRAINING YOU DO WHEN YOU ARE NOT TRAINING

For a long time I never had a horse that I could call mine. Ever since I began riding from about the age of eight I always rode horses that belonged to other people. It was never a problem because by the time I had reached thirteen or so people were always asking me to ride their horses. I even got to compete at a fairly high level on borrowed horses. By the time I was fifteen I was getting paid to break in, problem solve and train horses for other people. Getting paid meant to me that I was a "professional" and I figured that being a "professional" meant I was pretty good at this job. In these early stages of my "professional" career I worked under the watchful eye of Walt or Amos or sometimes both. But working horses was never quite a smooth as I would have liked. Whenever I was beginning to think I really knew what I was doing around horses, there was always a horse to come along and bring me down a peg or two.

The horse I'm thinking of for this particular story was a chestnut gelding called Stormy. Amos had been watching me work Stormy on a couple of occasions while he had pretended to be cleaning his saddle or raking a yard. A couple of weeks after I began working with Stormy, Amos and I were having a conversation. He asked me how I had been getting along with the gelding. I told him things were going ok. Amos then asked how Stormy felt in my hands. I had to admit that he leaned a little on the inside rein during the turns.

"Well matey, there might be a few things we can do about that," Amos said. We agreed to get together in a few days and work on a few things.

In the mean time I continued to persevere with what I had been doing to get Stormy's turns a little more soft, but all I got out of it was tired legs and a sore shoulder. After a few days, Amos showed up with a paint horse called Blanket during one my sessions with Stormy. He said it was good I had tried a few things on my own. Amos suggested I get my legs a little more under my centre of gravity and made me get off and adjust the fenders back about an inch. He also shortened the stirrups a hole. I thought this was all fine, but what about fixing Stormy's turns?

Amos then said, "Now matey, why don't we look at ya backup? It looked to me like ya was doin some plowin with them back feet. I'd never seen so much draggin since I was boy with one of pop's plow horses."

Amos showed me how to get the horse to prepare to shift back with just a lift of the rein. First one foot with one rein, then another foot with the other rein. It took a few minutes, but soon there was hardly any drag in the feet and Stormy was backing straight.

Amos then suggested we go out for a trail ride together. He had already saddled Blanket. I had already told Amos that Stormy was a little rushy on the trail and tended to jog a lot. I wasn't sure why we going out on the trail when Amos knew I wanted to work on softening Stormy's turns. But I figured Amos had forgotten - after all he was quite old and I knew enough to know that old people forget things sometimes. I decided to not worry about the turns just now and placate Amos' desire to help me with Stormy's jogging problem on the trail.

We weren't long out the gate when Stormy began to get a little energy up and started jogging to stay ahead of Blanket. My reaction to this was to shorten my reins and pull him back to a walk. As soon as he walked I released the reins. It only took a couple of steps before Stormy was jogging again and I had to use the reins to get him to walk again. The pattern continued to repeat itself for quite sometime and I figured I must have been doing ok since Amos made no comment. Finally Amos said something.

"How'd ya reckin it's goin, matey? Is it gettin any better?"

"I don't seem to be getting through to him at all, Amos," was my response.

"Well, why don't we try somethin else then? When ya feel him gettin a little energy like he was about to trot, I want ya to take the left rein to the left - like an open rein. Leave ya right rein alone. Bend him to the left. Start out slow and not too tight a bend. If he don't slow his feet, bend him tighter with the left rein only until his feet slow to a walk. When that happens let go of the left rein and let him go no matter where he's pointin. Then just let him drift back to the track - don't go driving him back to the track - just let him find it. As soon as he starts gettin his feet goin a little faster, do the same to the right rein. When his feet slow up, let go of the rein and let him find his way back to the track. Try to feel the energy before his feet get movin faster, then bring the rein to the side. Now give it a go."

I started out as Amos described, but Stormy seemed to get pretty upset when I used the rein.

"Now listen, matey. Think of three things. Don't bring the rein back to ya - take it to the side. Ya askin the front feet to step across and go where the rein is goin. Takin the rein back is gettin them back feet to step under which ain't what we want just yet. Next thing is to be slow with ya hands. You are too quick with ya hands and ya gettin ya horse to brace against them. Slow up. Don't worry that he is leavin the track and heading to the trees - he won't hit them - he'll slow up when he gets close to them if he ain't slowed before then. Last thing is to try to feel the energy buildin in ya horse before he starts to trot. When ya feel the energy, don't wait for the trot to happen, bend him before the trot and ya will find ya won't have to do so much and get a better result."

I practiced what Amos had been talking about. We ended up in the trees a few times. But Amos was right, we didn't hit any and Stormy did slow up as we got close. Several times I had to virtually bend Stormy into a circle before he quite jogging. But it must have taken no more than 10 minutes before Stormy would give a slight bend to a walk even before I got the rein around. Within another 10 minutes Stormy was settled into a relaxing walk no matter if Blanket and Amos were beside us, ahead of us or behind us. I was fairly impressed with the result and mentioned to

Amos how relaxed Stormy felt.

Then Amos got the bright idea that we should leave the track and head into the trees. He told me to follow him. The trees were pretty close together and several times my legs brushed up against one trunk in an effort to avoid another. I had to duck a few low branches and managed to leave Amos behind when Stormy shied at a three foot ant's nest. By the time Amos had caught up with us we were already late for getting home. On the way home Amos had me working on trot/walk transitions on Stormy - again using only one rein. It started out as a bit of a mess, but ended with a lot of softness. I was very pleased with the result. When we got home and I was about to dismount, Amos asked me to go into the arena and do a couple of serpentines. I didn't know why and told him that I thought Stormy had done enough work for today. He asked me to humour him. I rode Stormy into the arena and trotted a couple of three loop serpentines when Amos called out that it was enough. I had forgotten all about the problem with Stormy's turns until then.

"How'd them turns feel to ya, matey?"

"Good. Even great. I hardly had to do anything to get him to follow the turns," I replied.

"Mmm. We must have scared the brace right out of him when we passed that ant's nest," Amos said with a smirk on his face.

I didn't even know we had been working on the turns during the ride, but I later realized that everything Amos had me doing with adjusting the stirrups, the rein back and the trail work were more than they appeared to be. Amos was teaching me that softness, responsiveness, trust, confidence, balance, position and timing are all things that you work on all the time no matter what you are working on. If you are working on flying changes, you are still working on all those things. If you are working on how to approach a spread fence, you are working on all those things. If you are working on float loading, you are working on all those things. It took me many, many mistakes to learn that I should never sacrifice any of those essential elements in order the get the job done. They are the basics of everything we do with horses and any problem you have at higher levels are because of a problem you have with the essential basics of timing, feel, balance and position.

SOFTNESS
VERSUS LIGHTNESS

Is there a difference between a horse that is light and a horse that is soft? This was the question I pondered when asked by a friend why her horse was soft when handled on the ground, yet stiff and resistant when she rode him. It is an interesting question because I think many people have the same confusion. Many, many competition horses that I see are often light on the reins and light on the legs, but they are not soft. I have been often told by a rider that their horse is soft because he does not lean on the reins or they can work him off their seat alone with only a minimum input from the reins or legs. But when I have watched their horse I don't see softness. I only see responsiveness. So what is the difference?

When I was a teenager and began breaking horses my abilities were pretty raw. At first all my efforts were carefully guided by Walt and Amos, but as my skills grew so did the length of the leash that the old brothers gave me. One of the horses that came my way was called Checkers. She was a chestnut mare that stood about 15 hands. Although she was fairly braced up there was nothing to indicate she would give me much trouble. Any problems she had came from a lack of handling and not from poor handling.

Checkers took to the work pretty smoothly. She didn't understand what a hindquarter yield was about and she loved to lean on the rein through a back up. But overall she was a quick and willing learner. I found that she really didn't take well to much pressure. If I asked her to give to the rein, she often gave too much and got quite hurried in her steps. Her neck would brace and her back would hollow out. But this meant that I could ask with less pressure the next time and she got better. With regular work and consistency in my approach I was able to get good responses from Checkers with just the lightest requests.

Things were going really well up to the day I reckoned it was time to take Checkers out of the arena and go out for her first trail ride. We hadn't gone more than a few hundred metres out the gate before Checkers started to surge forward. I asked her to slow down with my reins, but all that did was get her to side pass along the trail without any slowing down of her feet. She was set on heading down the track as quickly as I would allow. I know better now, but at the time I felt I had to keep a tight rein on her to prevent her from bolting off on me. It was only a ten minute ride, but it was the longest ten minutes I had experienced in quite awhile.

When we had got back and I had unsaddled Checkers and put her away I started to worry about what had happened. I knew Checkers worked really nicely in the arena and I knew she understood about slowing to the rein and seat. But what good was all that if she didn't listen to me when she was out of the arena. I didn't understand at the time how a horse could be so responsive to me at home and totally ignore me at other times.

Later that day Walt was brushing his horse Ben after they had been out for a trail ride. We exchanged greetings and he asked me how I went with Checkers that morning. I told him what a pain she had been and I figured I would have to just get stronger with her next time.

"Don't be too hard on her, matey. It was her first ride out of the arena and it should be expected that she'd have the jiggers" he said.

"But Walt she would hardly listen to me at all. It was like I was on a different horse. I don't get it when she can be so soft in the arena," I complained.

"Well, maybe she ain't as soft as ya think."

I decided to correct Walt on this point. "But in the arena I can stop her from a trot with just my seat and turn her with the lightest aids I could give.

No, I reckon I've got her softer than any horse I have ever handled."

"D'ya reckon she's soft or is she just light," he asked?

That tone and that question! I knew I had just revealed my ignorance to Walt by saying something really stupid. I was about to get a lecture from the old man. I prepared myself and then asked the obvious.

"What d'ya mean?"

"Well ya can have a lot of lightness without much softness. I seen ya ridin Checkers in the arena and I don't see nearly as much softness as I do lightness in what ya got goin on with her. Ya see matey lightness just requires a horse submits to ya rein or ya legs or ya seat with her body. But to get softness she's gotta yield with her mind too. If ya don't have her yieldin with her mind there'll be times when the lightness won't be there - like ya found out today.

"You are losing me Walt. What do you mean?"

"Let's take Checkers for example. I seen ya ridin her. I seen ya get hindquarter yields and stops and forehand yields and upward transitions and downward transitions and so on and so on. I seen that ya got it to a stage where ya don't have to do a whole lot to get these things to happen. But I also seen how ya got this workin for ya. And I seen how Checkers feels about how ya got this workin for ya. I seen Checkers respond to these things lightly because she aint too happy about what will happen if she fails. So while her feet is doing what ya is askin, her mind is wishin she was somewhere else. If ya don't get this turned around, eventually when she gets in a bad spot her mind will take over her feet and ya won't be able to do too much about it. That's what happened this mornin."

This terrible dread came over me. I thought to myself "Oh my God, I've wrecked her." But Walt must have heard my thought.

"No, ya aint wrecked her. But if ya want it to be better ya gotta get her to keep checkin in with ya. When she asks ya a question, be there to give her an answer."

"What does that mean, Walt?"

"It means matey that if she asks ya if she can slow down but ya don't want her to slow down, just tell her with ya energy that maybe she can try to keep goin. But don't yell at her like ya been doin that she can't slow down. Even if she does slow down, don't demand that she keep goin. Ask

157

her if she can keep goin. Maybe even let her slow down sometimes, even though it may not have been what you wanted."

"But won't that teach her to just take over and do what she wants any time," I asked?

"If every time she asks to slow down or turn or whatever, ya say she can do what came into her mind, then ya will teach her to take over. But if ya keep changin your answer to her questions, then she won't. But ya gotta give her an answer - don't not answer her when she asks. It will help keep her mind focused on ya and she will keep checkin in and askin ya a question. Which means that she will try hard to be with ya and stay tuned in. Whenever Checkers is talkin to ya I noticed that ya kinda tune her out and don't answer her until she is doing somethin ya don't want. So Checkers has been learnin to tune you out too. Now it's got to the stage where if ya want to do anythin with her ya are interruptin some other thought she may be havin. She may be light on the aids, but she aint mentally light to the idea. If ya want to have a soft horse, you re going to have to take care of the response of her mind as well as the response of her body. Lightness is a physical response to them aids, but softness is an emotional response."

It has taken me years to understand what Walt had been trying to tell me. I'm not sure if I still understand much of it. It is a lot easier to see the difference between a horse that is light and one that is soft for me. But putting the softness in a horse is a lot more work than I realized all those years ago. There are three things I have learned. You can have lightness without softness, but you can't have softness without lightness. Many problems that people encounter are because most people mistake lightness for softness. Secondly, softness and lightness are not all or nothing things. They are not black and white. All horses have a degree of lightness and a degree of softness. Obtaining more softness in a horse is a path or journey. You may not start with much, but if you do the right thing as you travel along the path you achieve more and more softness. Of course, if you don't do the right thing you can put less and less softness in your horse too. Lastly, you never get to the end of the path. No horse and no rider ever lives long enough to achieve absolute softness and absolute lightness. But that doesn't mean you shouldn't keep striving to reach it.

THE LAST TIME
I SAW WALT

I can remember the last time I saw Walt. It was 1984. I had completed university studies and was about to head off to Canada to take up a job offer. Amos had died 3 years earlier and Walt had found it impossible to cope by himself. Six months after the death of Amos, Walt had been put into a government nursing home and that was where I found him. Walt and Amos had lived their whole lives together. They were together in their mother's womb and they stayed together until Amos died at the age of 85. Neither had married and I even wonder if either of them had ever had a girlfriend. But in many ways they were more married than most married couples. Walt and Amos were special. They had a gift. The gift of understanding through feel. They understood each other. They understood other people. And they understood horses. It was an innate understanding. They didn't learn it, they just felt it. Walt had aged considerably since I last saw him. He was even more wizened and leathery than I imagined possible. He had become frail and it seemed a strain for him to sit up in his chair. But at 88 he was still very sharp and recognized me immediately.

"Hey matey," was his greeting.

It was the way he had always greeted me ever since I was about 10 years old. I don't think he had ever called me Ross. We talked for nearly a couple of hours until the nurse came to get him for lunch. He asked about university and the job. We talked about my life. We talked lots about Amos and the old days at the riding school. We replayed some of the funny and not so funny incidents. I was amazed that his memory was so much better than mine. I reminded him of the only time I got furious with him and Amos. I've told this story before, but it was the time Walt and Amos decided I needed to be taught a lesson about asking a horse politely before I demand anything from him.

I had been riding a horse for another fellow. The horse was not very forward and I decided she needed to be kicked and kicked and kicked to get going forward. After a few days of this sort of riding she was getting no better. At the end of the day I asked Walt for a lift home in his old truck. He said that if I wanted a lift I first had to get his knife from his pocket. At the time I thought this was an odd game to play, but reminded myself that I was dealing with old men who liked to play silly games. I knew Walt carried one of those old pocket knives, so I went to reach for the knife in his jacket pocket. Walt had his hand in his pocket and I couldn't get at the knife. I pulled and pulled, but Walt didn't remove his hand and I could not reach the watch. I remember Walt said something like, "Well Tarzan, let's see if Amos can do it."

Amos then turned to Walt and asked if could borrow the pocket knife. At which Walt gently removed his knife from his pocket and hands it to Amos. He then turned back to me and let me know that I would have to walk home. All the way home I was fuming at these two old blokes playing a trick like that on me. But over the next couple of days the lesson finally began to sink in and I was able to apply what Walt and Amos had been trying to tell me about politeness to the little mare. I tried hard to stay mad at Walt, but as the mare got better my temper dissolved. Walt and I laughed about this in the nursing home that last day and he was glad I still remembered because he did too.

He was glad to hear the riding school was still there in bricks and mortar even though most of the people had long gone. It didn't take long to get around to talking about the inside of the horse, though. I guess it was to be expected, since what horses think and feel is the number one passion for both of us

"You know matey, there is two kinds of horsemen. The ones that think like people and the ones that think like horses. The ones that think like people are takers and the ones that think like horses are givers."

"Walt, you have never learned to speak English! What do you mean takers and givers," I asked?

"Well matey, it's the nature of people to take. That's what makes humans so successful. We take from ourselves and we take from others. We take and we take. We use what we can for our own reasons. The takers use horses for themselves. They use them 'cause they wanna go fast. They use them 'cause they want something from them. They take from the horse like they have a right to what the horse gives them. They take away the horse's right to run away. They take away the horses right to say no when he don't wanna do somethin. A giver gives back somethin to the horse. He don't take away the right of the horse to run away or to say no. He just sets it up so the horse don't wanna run away or don't wanna say no. The giver gives the horse the willingness to go along with the giver's idea, but he don't take away the right to say no. People who talk about dominance and submission are takers. People who talk about yielding and leadership are givers. If ya gonna be good with horses, ya need to be a giver cause that's what horses are. Horses are givers. They don't try to ever take away anythin from us. To get along good with a giver ya need to learn to be a giver too."

We talked some more about horses. Walt talked about what he meant by the spirit of the horse. Walt talked about his regret at not being able to live long enough to learn more about horses. And we talked about Amos. But he was getting tired and I knew by the time the nurse arrived to take him to lunch that it was time for me to go.

As I got up to leave Walt pointed to a little bedside cabinet. He said, "Open the second draw, will ya matey."

When I did I saw a few pens, some note paper, a comb and an ancient looking wooden box about the size of a cigarette pack.

"Matey, I want ya to take the box. There's somethin I've been keepin for ya that I want ya to have."

I opened the box and saw inside the old pocket knife. Walt knew and I knew that it was our last visit together. I will never be able to describe the intensity of emotion that I felt as I walked to the car park. I didn't even know until I sat inside my car that tears were streaming down my cheeks. About 18 months later I was visiting Finland for a conference when I got a phone call from my wife. She said there had been a call from mum that Walt had died 2 days earlier. I put my hand in my pocket and wrapped my fist around the knife. The greatest giver I had ever known had left me.

Lightning Source UK Ltd.
Milton Keynes UK
UKHW041837260319
339945UK00001B/48/P